The Trouble with America

The Trouble with America

Flawed Government, Failed Society

Kenneth J. Long

LEXINGTON BOOKS

A Division of
ROWMAN & LITTLEFIELD PUBLISHERS, INC.
Lanham • Boulder • New York • Toronto • Plymouth, UK

LEXINGTON BOOKS

A division of Rowman & Littlefield Publishers, Inc.
A wholly owned subsidiary of The Rowman & Littlefield Publishing Group, Inc.
4501 Forbes Boulevard, Suite 200
Lanham, MD 20706

Estover Road
Plymouth PL6 7PY
United Kingdom

British Library Cataloguing in Publication Information Available

Library of Congress Cataloging-in-Publication Data

Long, Kenneth J., 1958-
 The trouble with America : flawed government, failed society /
Kenneth J. Long.
   p. cm.
 Includes bibliographical references and index.
 ISBN-13: 978-0-7391-2830-5 (cloth : alk. paper)
 ISBN-13: 978-0-7391-2831-2 (pbk. : alk. paper)
 ISBN-13: 978-0-7391-3271-5 (electronic : alk. paper)
 ISBN-10: 0-7391-2830-2 (cloth : alk. paper)
 1. United States—Politics and government—Philosophy. 2. United
States—Social conditions. I. Title.
 JK275.L67 2008
 320.973—dc22   2008040461

Printed in the United States of America

∞™ The paper used in this publication meets the minimum requirements of
American National Standard for Information Sciences—Permanence of Paper
for Printed Library Materials, ANSI/NISO Z39.48-1992.

To my brilliant and beautiful wife, Anita, and in loving memory of my extraordinary parents, David and Rita.

Contents

List of Tables

HEALTH TABLES

SAFETY TABLES

EDUCATION TABLES

OPPORTUNITY TABLES

REPRESENTATION TABLES

Preface

This is an unusual little book. I wrote it hoping that it might be useful as an ancillary text for courses on American government and politics: the introduction to American government course especially, but also perhaps courses in political theory, public policy, foreign policy, law, state and local government, public administration and maybe even some courses outside the discipline of Political Science concerned with problems of American politics. Of course, I also hoped that this book might be of interest to those who are "students" only in the functional sense of the word—not enrolled in any course but looking for a better understanding of why American politics so often seems plagued by paralysis, unable to generate satisfactory public solutions to our public problems and rarely evocative of our better angels. Ancillary texts, however, are not pervasively used in American politics courses. The standard introduction to American politics text is fairly lengthy and, in an era when college and university students are generally not required to read as much as they were two or three generations ago, there isn't a lot of time for additional required reading. That is why this unusual little book is little. I want it to be brief enough to be practical to use in most American politics courses.

Of the ancillary texts that are still most commonly required, most seem to be casebooks or anthologies—collections of competing perspectives on key issues or policies—and instructors can pick and choose among their various entries in assigning required reading. Too often, however, these anthologies seem to imply that there are only two major perspectives on most matters: one conservative and one liberal or, conceptualized a bit differently, one Republican and one Democratic. It is my belief, however, that students are best engaged in more thoughtful consideration of politics when they encounter strong opinions and partisan arguments that are less familiar to them than mainstream fare of one kind or another, arguments that question the political institutions and beliefs which are foundational in America. Too often, American government texts strive to be "objective" only to retain considerable bias, namely, the centrist bias of identifying one position slightly left of center, one slightly right of center, and then suggesting that the "truth" may lie anywhere between the two.

My ancillary text is a bit different. In it, I am arguing that America fails not because we have deviated from, or failed to live up to, our founding principles and the core political structures that were built to protect them, but rather because we have remained true to these principles and structures. It will be the rare reader who agrees with all the claims made here and it is my expectation that this book will be as useful to those who disagree most of the time as it is to those inclined to agree most of the time. I do not think of this book as ideological. Although my ideological leanings may be best described as socialist, I cannot and do not speak for all socialists and certainly not for all leftists. Indeed, in this book, I often cite with great admiration the arguments of those from a wide variety of ideological leanings including anarchist, green, liberal, and even conservative.

Because I question so much in so few pages, this book is almost certainly a better place to begin an exploration of American government and politics than to conclude one. To some extent, I am playing with ideas in the pages that follow, asking questions more than answering them. This book is intentionally provocative; it is meant to lead to discussions and ideas far beyond those addressed here. For example, I make some references to quotes from Jean Baudrillard in my chapter on capitalism but, in the interest of brevity and simplicity, nowhere do I explain his philosophy. Nor do I present any postmodern critique of American society as he did so creatively. In short, my goal of presenting a brief and simple critique of American government, one suitable for inclusion in introductory courses structured largely around chunky standard textbooks, precluded me from drawing out all the ideas I touch upon as fully as they may go. Still, what follows, I hope, is an invitation to question American politics more seriously and to explore it further. I also hope it provides some basic insight into how terribly far from good government we in America have always been and currently remain.

As I write this, the 2008 presidential election is gearing up and, true to the problems of American "leadership" discussed in chapter four, Senator Barack Obama is running on slogans that promise "change you can believe in" and "change we need," having defeated Senators Hillary Clinton and John Edwards, who had slogans that were nearly identical. Now, at a time when economic and war woes considerably advantage his party, he is about to test the depths of American racism by taking on Senator John McCain who, despite becoming the nominee of the party incumbent to the White House, is also running as the candidate of change. However, despite all this talk of change, despite how desperately it seems needed, substantive positive change anytime soon seems as unlikely as ever.

West Hartford, Connecticut
August 2008

Acknowledgments

I would like to thank my wife, Anita Durkin, for providing important and always helpful editorial assistance. My friend and fellow Political Scientist, Harald Sandstrom, read early drafts of the first couple of chapters and provided several useful suggestions for improvement. At Saint Joseph College, I wish to thank those who, in service of my classroom needs, provided assistance that spilled over into enriching this book: work-study student Lisa Nguyen, librarians Kathleen Kelley, Lynne Piacentini, Antoinette Collins, and especially Sheila Martin, all of whom helped locate key resources, and my secretary, Pat Senich, who provided very helpful secretarial assistance, and work-study student Khristina Surgeon who helped with the final phase of proofreading.

Introduction:
Where the Trouble Lies

The overwhelming majority of Americans believe that the United States is the best country ever. This pride in America is prevalent not just among ordinary Americans but among our politicians and Political Scientists as well. Yet most of us Americans do not have much faith in each other, our government, or our leaders. Public opinion polls consistently reveal that far more of us have very little confidence in our government and politicians than the very small percentage who have a great deal of confidence in our government and politicians. Similarly, many more of us have little confidence in the political wisdom of the American people than those who have a lot of confidence in it.

But if we don't have much confidence in our countrywomen and countrymen, our government, or our politicians (together these may be the essence of any country), what is it that inspires our confidence that America is the best country anywhere? It would be strange if America's greatness was considered to be only its geographic assets, national wealth, or military prowess and yet that would seem to be all we have to celebrate. It may be likely that most Americans are proud of our freedom from our own government, proud of the weakness of our government compared to the world's many tyrannies. However, as we will see in this book, our Constitution mostly secures capitalist property protection. It does not protect the freedom of ordinary Americans close to our level of expectation, even in a post-9/11 environment wherein we anticipate that our freedom will be compromised at least a little.

The United States is a very troubled country. We have a people who are not particularly virtuous, a political system that is distressingly weak and ineffectual, and politicians who rarely exhibit anything approaching leadership or statesmanship. We do not even have a particularly good country, let alone the best one on the planet. To be sure, America is not a terrible place. Other countries have tyrants that slaughter large segments of their own citizenry. That doesn't happen here. Other countries endure wide-scale crushing poverty, millions starving to death, raw sewage running through the streets, political instability, and violent civil warfare. Those things are almost unimaginable here. Instead, America is the wealthiest country in the world. What could be wrong with that? American movie actress and iconic figure Mae West was famous for films in the 1930s and '40s, and once said, "I've been rich and I've been poor and rich is better." She was right, at least to the extent that affluence creates comfort and poverty does not. And yet, America is nonetheless troubled. How can a country that has so much fall so far short of its potential? Many other countries, with far less wealth, have done much more than we have to assure the health, safety, education, opportunity, and representation of their people. And while these may not be the only things that people hope their government can safeguard, I doubt that a country can be truly great if it doesn't measure up in its ability to keep its people safe, promote their health, facilitate their learning and their hopes for success and growth, and respond to their other wishes by representing their will.

It is very easy to argue about how to best interpret and measure such things as the health, safety, education, opportunity, and representation of people. This book will give some attention to such matters. But for now, just to begin to get acquainted with some of the highlights of the failures of America, take a look at the indices and rankings in Tables 1 through 11. These statistics are not the only indices that can be used to see how the United States compares with other countries. No statistic, including any of these, can distill the essence of America and these are not necessarily the only comparisons that matter. They are also not the statistics that reveal America in the harshest light. Rather, these tables are presented simply because they are a logical place to look to get a reasonable introductory glimpse of how our country compares to others in its ability to deliver the conditions which meet people's needs and wants.

Tables 1 and 2 both address issues of health. Table 1 (Infant Mortality) reveals that the United States recently ranked 41st in the world for low infant mortality. At first glance, this may not seem all that bad until one realizes that not just Western European countries rank ahead of us but so do many third world nations. Sweden and Japan have infant mortality rates less than half as large as ours. The primary reasons for our relatively poor ranking, despite such superiority in wealth and medical facilities, are well known: the failure of our government to adequately subsidize prenatal health care for the poor and the relative stinginess with which we attempt to mitigate poverty in general. Without decent living conditions and read-

Table 1. Lowest Infant Mortality Rates

Rank	Country	Infant Mortality Rate (per 1,000)	Rank	Country	Infant Mortality Rate (per 1,000)
1	Singapore	2.30	26	Portugal	4.92
2	Sweden	2.76	27	Gibraltar	4.98
3	Japan	2.80	28	United Kingdom	5.01
4	Hong Kong	2.94	29	Jersey	5.08
5	Iceland	3.27	30	Ireland	5.22
6	France	3.41	31	Monaco	5.27
7	Finland	3.52	32	Greece	5.34
8	Norway	3.64	33	San Marino	5.53
9	Malta	3.82	34	Taiwan	5.54
10	Czech Republic	3.86	35	New Zealand	5.67
11	Andorra	4.03	36	Man, Isle of	5.72
12	Germany	4.08	36	Italy	5.72
13	Switzerland	4.28	38	Faroe Islands	6.01
14	Spain	4.31	39	Cuba	6.04
15	Macau	4.33	40	Korea, South	6.05
16	Slovenia	4.35	**41**	**United States**	**6.37**
17	Denmark	4.45	42	Croatia	6.60
18	Austria	4.54	43	Belarus	6.63
19	Belgium	4.56	44	Guam	6.68
20	Australia	4.57	44	Lithuania	6.68
21	Liechtenstein	4.58	46	Israel	6.75
22	Guernsey	4.59	47	Northern Mariana Islands	6.85
23	Canada	4.63	48	Montserrat	7.03
24	Luxembourg	4.68	49	Poland	7.07
25	Netherlands	4.88	50	Slovakia	7.12

Source: Drawn from data in the Central Intelligence Agency, *The CIA World Factbook, 2007*, New York: Skyhorse Publishing, 2006.

ily affordable health care for everyone, far too many American infants are susceptible to fatal yet preventable conditions.

Table 2 (Life Expectancy) shows that the last decennial World Health Organization report indicated that the United States ranked 24th among countries in life expectancy. Again, the vast majority of Western European countries rank ahead of us (all except Cyprus, Denmark, Ireland, and Portugal) in spite of the much higher smoking rates in these countries. *Wealthy* Americans may live relatively long lives, but our country as a whole ranks comparatively poorly because we do not do as much to safeguard the health and safety of our poorer classes. Overall, Americans die earlier and spend more time disabled than do members of nearly all other advanced countries.

Table 2.   Longest Life Expectancies

Rank	Country	Disability Adjusted Life Expectancy	Rank	Country	Disability Adjusted Life Expectancy
1	Japan	74.5	16	Belgium	71.6
2	Australia	73.2	17	Austria	71.6
3	France	73.1	18	Luxembourg	71.1
4	Sweden	73.0	19	Iceland	70.8
5	Spain	72.8	20	Finland	70.5
6	Italy	72.7	21	Malta	70.5
7	Greece	72.5	22	Germany	70.4
8	Switzerland	72.5	23	Israel	70.4
9	Monaco	72.4	**24**	**United States**	**70.0**
10	Andorra	72.3	25	Cyprus	69.8
11	San Marino	72.3	26	Dominica	69.8
12	Canada	72.0	27	Ireland	69.6
13	Netherlands	72.0	28	Denmark	69.4
14	United Kingdom	71.7	29	Portugal	69.3
15	Norway	71.7	30	Singapore	69.3

Source: World Health Organization, *The World Health Report 2000*, Health Systems, Geneva: World Health Organization, 2000, pp. 34–41.

Tables 3 and 4 address issues of personal safety. In these tables, the United States is ranked among the worst in the world. In table 3 (Murder Rate), the United States was recently ranked as being the 24th *most* murderous country in the world. For perspective, keep in mind that our murder rate is more than nine times higher than those of Finland, Ireland, or Japan. It is more than twice as high as the Western European average. The principal reasons for this embarrassing statistic may include our relatively high rate of poverty, the paucity of gun control measures, and, according to many, a culture that champions violence in many aspects, from boxing and football to movies and video games.

Our rape rate is indicated in table 4 as the 9th *worst* in the world. Since rape may well be the most underreported crime in the world, and in many countries it is not always even a crime, it is hard to know what portion of this ranking stems from differential rates of crime reporting. Nonetheless, the United States is often regarded an especially unsafe place for women and children. American sociological estimates of the portion of women who are raped at least once in their lifetime and of children who are molested at least once during childhood range from about one in four to perhaps approaching one in three. Possible reasons for this disturbing level of sexual abuse include the effects of a relatively puritanical culture (trying to suppress human sexuality can foster pathology), widespread male reaction against feminist

Table 3. Highest Murder Rates

Rank	Country	Murders (per 100,000 people)	Rank	Country	Murders (per 100,000 people)
1	Colombia	61.78	16	Zimbabwe	7.50
2	South Africa	49.60	17	Seychelles	7.39
3	Jamaica	32.42	18	Zambia	7.08
4	Venezuela	31.61	19	Costa Rica	6.10
5	Russia	20.15	20	Poland	5.63
6	Mexico	13.02	21	Georgia	5.11
7	Estonia	10.73	22	Uruguay	4.51
8	Latvia	10.39	23	Bulgaria	4.46
9	Lithuania	10.29	**24**	**United States**	**4.28**
10	Belarus	9.83	25	Armenia	4.26
11	Ukraine	9.40	26	India	3.44
12	Papua New Guinea	8.39	27	Yemen	3.36
13	Kyrgyzstan	8.03	28	Dominica	2.90
14	Thailand	8.01	29	Azerbaijan	2.86
15	Moldova	7.81	30	Finland	2.83

Source: Centre for International Crime Prevention, *Seventh United Nations Survey of Crime Trends & Operations of Criminal Justice Systems,* New York: United Nations Office on Drugs and Crime, 2007.

gains in other aspects of society, relatively lax and poorly enforced laws against rape and molestation, and the general violence of America (which may be associated with both poverty and sexism).

Recent statistical indicators of education in America also suggest that we fall far short of being anywhere near the best in the world at educating our

Table 4. Highest Rape Rates

Rank	Country	Rapes (per 100,000 people)	Rank	Country	Rapes (per 100,000 people)
1	South Africa	119.54	11	Papua New Guinea	23.35
2	Seychelles	78.83	12	New Zealand	21.34
3	Australia	77.80	13	United Kingdom	14.22
4	Montserrat	74.94	14	Spain	14.04
5	Canada	73.31	15	France	13.94
6	Jamaica	47.66	16	South Korea	12.62
7	Zimbabwe	45.78	17	Mexico	12.30
8	Dominica	34.77	18	Norway	12.08
9	**United States**	**30.13**	19	Costa Rica	11.83
10	Iceland	24.60	20	Venezuela	11.55

Source: Centre for International Crime Prevention, *Seventh United Nations Survey of Crime Trends & Operations of Criminal Justice Systems,* New York: United Nations Office on Drugs and Crime, 2007.

people. Our rudimentary literacy rate of 99 percent placed us tied for 24th in the world (see table 5). We are not among the dozen or so countries with universal or virtually universal literacy. If literacy is defined as an ability to read and write more than the simplest sentences, our relative standing in the world is even less impressive. We pay great lip service to the importance of educating our society and education receives enormous emphasis in American political campaigns at all levels from federal to local. Even so, together our federal, state, and local governments expended a smaller portion of our resource on education than did 37 other countries and territories (see table 6). In America, free public education stops at grade twelve and the best schools are nearly always the private ones. The onerous costs of colleges and universities are borne primarily by students themselves and the general availability of student loans is of little use to students from families that depend on them to provide a *continuous* source of income to keep the family afloat. Again, America has some fabulous facilities, some wonderful educational institutions, but it does a relatively poor job of making them accessible to the bulk of the population.

Table 5. Literacy Rates (with literacy defined as the ability to read and write a simple sentence)

Rank	Country	Literacy	Rank	Country	Literacy
1	Georgia	100	23	Moldova	99.10
1	Finland	100	24	United Kingdom	99.00
1	Greenland	100	**24**	**United States**	**99.00**
1	Vatican City	100	24	France	99.00
1	Luxembourg	100	24	Germany	99.00
1	Liechtenstein	100	24	Guam	99.00
1	Norway	100	24	Iceland	99.00
1	Andorra	100	24	Japan	99.00
9	Estonia	99.80	24	Ireland	99.00
9	Latvia	99.80	24	Korea, North	99.00
9	Poland	99.80	24	Monaco	99.00
12	Ukraine	99.70	24	Netherlands	99.00
12	Barbados	99.70	24	New Zealand	99.00
12	Slovenia	99.70	24	Belgium	99.00
12	Samoa	99.70	24	Australia	99.00
16	Lithuania	99.60	24	Denmark	99.00
16	Russia	99.60	24	Czech Republic	99.00
16	Belarus	99.60	24	Canada	99.00
16	Slovakia	99.60	24	Switzerland	99.00
20	Hungary	99.40	24	St. Pierre & Miquelon	99.00
20	Tajikistan	99.40	24	Sweden	99.00
22	Uzbekistan	99.30			

Source: Drawn from data in the Central Intelligence Agency, *The CIA World Factbook, 2007,* New York: Skyhorse Publishing, 2006.

Table 6.   Government Educational Expenditures as Percentage of Gross National Product

Rank	Country	Public Expenditures on Education as % of GNP	Rank	Country	Public Expenditures on Education as % of GNP
1	Cuba	18.7	24	Tunisia	6.4
2	Vanuatu	11	25	Bolivia	6.3
3	Lesotho	10.4	26	Cyprus	6.3
4	St. Vincent & Gren.	10	27	Belgium	6.3
5	Yemen	9.5	28	Slovenia	6.1
6	Brunel	9.1	29	Jamaica	6.1
7	Mongolia	9	30	Malawi	6
8	Denmark	8.5	31	Belarus	6
9	Guyana	8.4	32	Iceland	6
10	Malaysia	8.1	33	Lithuania	5.9
11	Cape Verde	7.9	34	Latvia	5.8
12	St. Lucia	7.7	35	Portugal	5.8
13	Sweden	7.7	36	Switzerland	5.8
14	St. Kitts & Nevis	7.6	37	Austria	5.7
15	Barbados	7.6	**38**	**United States**	**5.7**
16	Norway	7.6	39	Estonia	5.7
17	Israel	7.5	40	Fiji	5.6
18	Namibia	7.2	41	Poland	5.6
19	Swaziland	7.1	42	France	5.6
20	Kenya	7	43	Hungary	5.5
21	New Zealand	6.7	44	Ireland	5.5
22	Morocco	6.5	45	Ukraine	5.4
23	Finland	6.4			

Source: United Nations Development Programme, *Human Development Report 2007/2008,* New York: Palgrave Macmillan, 2007, pp. 265–68.

As Americans, we regularly take pride in living in what we generally perceive to be the land of opportunity. There is unparalleled wealth in this country but it is extraordinarily unequally distributed. So much so, apparently, that for working class Americans, there is actually *less* opportunity for economic advancement than what is found in other developed countries. Data on economic mobility is typically very hard to come by. Longitudinal studies are generally needed to track earnings over time. Nonetheless, there is ample evidence that, among developed nations, the United States has long had, and continues to have, among the *lowest* levels of economic opportunity and mobility for poor and working class citizens. Table 7 summarizes the findings of a landmark longitudinal comparison of the earnings mobility of low-paid workers in eight developed countries. The United States ranked *last* among the eight in all regards. Compared to these other

Table 7. Earnings Mobility of Low-Paid Workers in Eight Select Countries

		1991 earnings status of 1986 low-paid* workers			
Rank	Country	No longer Employed Full-Time	Still Low Paid*	Moved to Second Fifth	Moved to Upper 60%
1	United Kingdom	12.9	35.8	27.8	23.6
2	Italy	8.3	43.6	25.1	22.8
3	Finland	26.3	28.8	20.1	24.8
4	France	22.5	35.7	23.8	18.0
5	Denmark	26.7	32.1	20.5	20.7
6	Sweden	27.6	35.5	18.4	18.4
7	Germany	39.3	27.4	16.8	16.6
8	**United States**	**41.4**	**30.6**	**16.7**	**11.3**

*the bottom 20% of workers
Source: Organization for Economic Cooperation and Development, *Employment Outlook*, Paris: OECD, 1996, reported in Lawrence Mishel, Jared Bernstein, and John Schmitt, *The State of Working America, 2000/2001*, Ithaca, NY: ILR Press, 2001, p. 386.

countries, a smaller percentage of our low-paid workers moved from the bottom one-fifth of wage earners to either the second lowest one-fifth or above. In fact, economic mobility of low-wage earners to the upper 60 percent of wage earners was more than twice as great in Finland and the United Kingdom than in the United States. A far higher percentage of our low-paid workers actually lost ground, as a result of losing full-time employment.

Table 8 compares the intergenerational mobility of citizens of six select countries. Again, the United States places a distant *last*—with the daughters and especially sons of our poorest one-fifth of the population decidedly more likely to stay poor than their counterparts elsewhere in the world. Table 9 reports the findings of another key longitudinal study—this one examining the effects of taxes and government transfer programs (such as public assistance and unemployment insurance benefits) on poverty rates in 15 developed countries. Of these countries, the United States clearly does the least to alleviate poverty. Our taxes are relatively regressive (they help the rich at the expense of the poor) and our public assistance programs are remarkably uncharitable. We reduce poverty at *less than half* the average rate of the other 14 countries surveyed. Consequently, our poverty rate remains *more than twice* as high as the average of the other countries. Of course, in 1996, the United States even further reduced its public assistance spending by replacing Aid to Families with Dependent Children (AFDC) with Temporary Assistance to Needy Families (TANF). The longitudinal data in tables 7 through 9 cover time periods pre-dating this change and thus actually *over*estimate economic mobility in America. America may be a fabulous

Table 8.   Intergenerational Mobility In Six Select Countries: Percent of Daughters and Sons in Lowest Fifth, Given Fathers in Lowest Fifth

Rank	Country	Daughters	Sons
1	Denmark	23.5%	24.7%
2	Sweden	23.9%	25.8%
3	Finland	23.8%	27.8%
4	Norway	23.5%	28.2%
5	United Kingdom	23.2%	30.3%
6	**United States**	**25.6%**	**42.2%**

Source: Markus Jäntti, Bernt Bratsberg, Knut Röed, Oddbjörn Raaum, Robin Naylor, Eva Österbacka, Anders Björklund, and Tor Eriksson, 2006, "American exceptionalism in a new light: A comparison of intergenerational earnings mobility in the Nordic countries, the United Kingdom, and the United States." Discussion Paper No. 1938, Bonn, Germany: Institute for the Study of Labor, 2006. Cited in Lawrence Mishel, Jared Bernstein, and Sylvia Allegretto, *The State of Working America, 2006/2007*, Ithaca, NY: ILR Press, 2007, p. 102.

place for the rich to get richer (at the apparent expense of others) but that is not what one normally thinks of when conceptualizing a "land of opportunity." Our child poverty rates are scandalous—in both absolute terms and in comparison to the other countries. Worse still, our transfer programs and taxes do far less to alleviate child poverty than any of the other 15

Table 9.   The Impact of Taxes and Transfers on Poverty Rates* in Fifteen Select Countries

		All Persons		
Rank	Country	Pre**	Post**	Change (%)
1	Belgium	28.4	5.5	−80.6
2	Sweden	34.1	6.7	−80.4
3	Denmark	26.9	7.5	−72.1
4	Netherlands	22.8	6.7	−70.6
5	Norway	21.8	6.6	−69.7
6	Germany	22.0	7.6	−65.5
7	France	21.6	7.5	−65.3
8	Italy	18.4	6.5	−64.7
9	Ireland	30.3	11.1	−63.4
10	Spain	28.2	10.4	−63.1
11	Finland	15.6	6.2	−60.3
12	Canada	23.4	11.7	−50.0
13	United Kingdom	29.2	14.6	−50.0
14	Australia	23.2	12.9	−44.4
15	**United States**	**26.7**	**19.1**	**−28.5**
Average excluding U.S.		23.8	9.2	−61.7

Source: Timothy M. Smeeding, "Financial Poverty in Developed Countries: The Evidence from LIS," *Luxembourg Income Study Working Paper No. 155*, 1997 cited in Lawrence Mishel, Jared Bernstein, and John Schmitt, *The State of Working America, 2000–2001*, Ithaca, NY: ILR Press, 2001, p. 394.
* Measured as share below 50% of the median adjusted disposable personal income for individuals.
** "Pre" refers to pre-tax, pre-transfer income; "post" refers to post-tax, post-transfer income.

Table 10.   Child Poverty Rates before and after Taxes and Transfers in Sixteen Select Countries, 2000.

Rank	Country	Before	After
1	Denmark	11.8	2.4
2	Finland	18.1	2.8
3	Norway	15.5	3.4
4	Sweden	18.0	4.2
5	Switzerland	7.8	6.8
6	France	27.7	7.5
7	Belgium	16.7	7.7
8	Netherlands	11.1	9.8
9	Germany	18.2	10.2
10	Austria	17.7	10.2
11	Canada	22.8	14.9
12	United Kingdom	25.4	15.4
13	Portugal	16.4	15.6
14	Ireland	24.9	15.7
15	New Zealand	27.9	16.3
16	**United States**	**26.6**	**21.9**
Average excluding U.S.		21.1	10.7

Source: Miles Corak and Wen-Hao Chen, *Child Poverty in Rich Countries, 2005*, Florence, Italy: UNICEF Innocenti Research Centre, 2005. Cited in Lawrence Mishel, Jared Bernstein, and Sylvia Allegretto, *The State of Working America, 2006/2007*, Ithaca, NY: ILR Press, 2007, p. 351.

countries assessed in Table 10. Our after tax and transfer child poverty rate is a whopping 21.9 percent (more than nine times worse than Denmark's rate of 2.4 percent and more than twice as bad as the other 15 countries' average rate: 10.7 percent).

The ultimate flaw in our political representation may stem from the gridlock generated by our political system of checks and balances. It is designed to prevent tyranny (and it does), but it also has the effect of preventing most significant changes of any sort, thereby disenfranchising all of us to the extent that we want such changes. This will be the focus of chapter 1. Even if American government did respond more readily to the will of the majority, however, there is still ample evidence pointing to some serious inadequacies in both the process and product of our system of representation. The process of our elections is marred by the role of big money, the absence of significant campaign finance reform, political campaigns that focus on sound bites rather than a substantive exploration of issues, and politicians who better resemble followers than leaders. Consider also how our electoral process is marred by embarrassingly low voter turnout rates (table 11). I suppose that some might wish to argue that non-voting is a sign of contentment, that if our government deviates too far from what the people want, turnout will increase. However, voting rates are lowest among the poorest and least educated. As we will see later, these are hardly the most content segments of our population. Rather than satisfaction, non-voting seems to reflect alienation from the process, which may stem from apathy, ignorance, disgust with American politics, or perhaps even an accurate impression that no matter who wins our elections, relatively little seems to improve as a result.

The product of our elections is the batch of almost exclusively Democratic and Republican politicians, mostly centrists, who win office here. If they indeed represent us, it would have to be with their actions as officeholders. They are not, in themselves, representative of the diversity of our country. As a group, they are very disproportionately white, male, and rich compared to our general population. Table 12 reveals that American voters

Table 11. Highest and Lowest Average Voter Turnout Rates in National Legislative Elections During the 1990s (of 163 Countries Holding Elections)

Vote as a percentage of the voting age population.					
Highest Turnout Rates			*Lowest Turnout Rates*		
Rank	Country	Vote/VAP %	Rank	Country	Vote/VAP %
1	Malta	96.7	163	Mali	27.1
2	Uruguay	96.1	162	Senegal	27.1
3	Cambodia	90.5	161	Egypt	27.7
4	Seychelles	90.2	160	Djibouti	28.0
5	Indonesia	90.2	159	Guatemala	29.6
6	Italy	90.2	158	Jordan	30.6
7	Angola	88.3	157	Zambia	32.0
8	Iceland	88.3	156	Guinea-Bissau	32.1
9	Uzbekistan	86.2	155	Colombia	33.8
10	Antigua & Barbuda	85.6	154	Burkina Faso	34.0
11	South Africa	85.5	153	Niger	35.6
12	Albania	85.3	152	Sudan	36.2
13	Greece	84.7	151	Yemen	36.8
14	Belgium	84.1	150	Sierra Leone	36.8
15	Israel	83.2	149	Zimbabwe	37.3
16	Czech Republic	82.8	148	Switzerland	37.7
17	Bosnia/Herzegovina	82.8	147	Singapore	39.4
18	Australia	82.7	146	Pakistan	39.8
19	Sweden	82.6	145	Ivory Coast	39.9
20	Azerbaijan	82.5	144	Mauritania	42.5
21	Kuwait	82.5	143	Haiti	42.9
22	Mongolia	82.3	142	Kenya	43.8
23	St. Lucia	82.0	141	Botswana	44.6
24	Western Samoa	81.9	**140**	**United States**	**44.9**
25	Denmark	81.7	139	Chad	45.1

Source: The International Institute for Democracy and Electoral Assistance, *Voter Turnout: A Global Survey*, Stockholm: International IDEA, 1998.

elect remarkably few women compared to the voters of other countries. Certainly, it is not that American women are less qualified than women of other parts of the world are; more likely, the biased outcome of American elections seems to reflect a fundamental flaw in the representative nature of our political process itself. Rich, white men still have remarkable advantages in the spheres of privilege, money, connections, and cultural stereotypes that collectively constitute American politics.

All of these various statistical tables are intended to act merely as an introduction to the trouble with America. For a country of unparalleled wealth, America still manages to rank disturbingly low on central measures of the basic success of countries (in general, those that reflect the level of their ability to take care of their people and to represent, and respond to, their wants and needs). Overall, our health, safety, education, opportunity, and representation seem nowhere near the very best in the world. *Some* Americans may have world-class health-care, education, etc., but too many Americans appear to be left out or left behind. When we look at America as a whole, we see a surprisingly troubled country. The trouble with America is not that it is anywhere near the worst place in the world; the trouble with America is that, despite our enormous fortune, America is not among the very best.

In many ways, this book is inspired by, and loosely patterned on, the brief political polemic of famed and award winning Nigerian novelist Chinua Achebe: *The Trouble with Nigeria*. Achebe is one of Africa's most popular and influential writers. Many consider him to be one of the best novelists anywhere currently writing in English. He has a strong sense of politics and his first and best known novel, *Things Fall Apart*, provides a powerful yet delicate critique of British colonialism in Africa. In 1983, he wrote the delightfully candid critique of his native country, *The Trouble with Nigeria*, to help explain why a nation of such enormous potential is such a constant disappointment. Upon winning its independence in 1960 and for years since, Nigeria was long considered the best hope, among African countries, for genuine democracy and economic prosperity. Americans were especially enamored of Nigeria because its constitution was explicitly patterned on that of the United States. Their constitution created pluralism, checks and balances, states, and federalism just like we have. Nigeria was also a country of sufficient size and resource to be a likely success. Even before independence, in the 1950s, huge oil reserves, some of the largest in the world, were discovered in Nigeria. What more could one ask for?

Unfortunately, however, Nigeria has been anything but successful. In 1966, the army took over the government. The following year, the eastern region of the country attempted to secede, proclaiming a new republic of Biafra. The military regime blockaded the rebels to starve them into submission. It worked. About two and a half years and about one million

Table 12. Share of Seats Held by Women in National Legislatures

Rank	Country	Lower/Single House %W	Upper House %W	Rank	Country	Lower/Single House %W	Upper House %W
1	Rwanda	4.8	34.6	45	United Arab Emirates	22.4	17.4
2	Sweden	47.3	—	46	Philippines	22.4	17.4
3	Finland	42.0	—	47	Bulgaria	21.1	—
4	Costa Rica	38.6	—	48	Eritrea	22.0	—
5	Norway	37.9	—	48	Senegal	22.0	40.0
6	Denmark	36.9	—	50	Ethiopia	21.9	18.8
7	Netherlands	36.7	34.7	51	Estonia	21.8	—
8	Cuba	36.0	—	51	Republic of Moldova	21.8	—
9	Spain	36.0	23.2	53	Croatia	21.7	—
10	Mozambique	34.8	—	54	Pakistan	21.3	17.0
11	Belgium	34.7	38.0	54	Portugal	21.3	—
12	South Africa	32.9	33.3	56	Canada	20.8	35.0
13	Austria	32.2	27.4	56	Monaco	20.8	—
14	New Zealand	32.2	—	58	Poland	20.4	8.0
15	Iceland	31.7	—	58	Serbia	20.4	—
16	Germany	31.6	21.7	60	China	20.3	—
17	Burundi	30.5	34.7	61	North Korea	20.1	—
18	Tanzania	30.4	—	62	Dominican Republic	19.7	3.1
19	Uganda	29.8	—	62	United Kingdom	19.7	18.9
20	Switzerland	29.5	16.7	64	Trinidad and Tobago	19.4	32.3
21	Peru	29.2	—	65	Guinea	19.3	—

(continued)

Table 12. (continued)

Rank	Country	Lower/Single House %W	Upper House %W	Rank	Country	Lower/Single House %W	Upper House %W
22	Belarus	29.1	31.0	65	Slovakia	19.3	—
23	Guyana	29.0	—	67	Latvia	19.0	—
24	Andorra	28.6	—	68	Venezuela	18.6	—
25	Macedonia	28.3	—	69	France	18.5	16.9
26	Timor-Leste	27.7	—	69	Nicaragua	18.5	—
27	Afghanistan	27.3	22.5	71	St. Vincent & Gren.	18.2	—
28	Namibia	26.9	26.9	72	Sudan	18.1	—
29	Grenada	26.7	30.8	73	Equatorial Guinea	18.0	—
30	Viet Nam	25.8	—	74	Mauritania	17.9	17.9
31	Iraq	25.5	—	75	Tajikistan	17.5	23.5
31	Suriname	25.5	—	75	Uzbekistan	17.5	15.0
33	Laos	25.2	—	77	Italy	17.3	13.7
34	Ecuador	25.0	—	77	Nepal	17.3	—
35	Lithuania	24.8	—	79	Mauritius	17.1	—
36	Australia	24.7	35.5	80	Bolivia	16.9	3.7
37	Singapore	24.5	—	81	El Salvador	16.7	—
38	Liechtenstein	24.0	—	81	Panama	16.7	—
39	Lesotho	23.5	30.3	81	Zimbabwe	16.7	34.8
40	Seychelles	23.5	—	84	United States	16.3	6.0
41	Honduras	23.4	—	85	Greece	16.0	—
42	Luxembourg	23.3	—	85	Turkmenistan	16.0	—
43	Tunisia	22.8	13.4	87	Kazakhstan	15.9	4.3
44	Mexico	22.6	17.2	88	Czech Republic	15.5	14.8

Source: Women in National Parliaments, Geneva, Switzerland: Inter-Parliamentary Union, 2007. See www.ipu.org/wmn-e/classif.htm.

starvation deaths later, Biafran rebels capitulated and Nigerian national unity was preserved. In 1979, civilian rule was reestablished but, within four years (1983), the military took over again. Even the military regimes were unstable. A third military coup occurred in 1985. In 1993, the military attempted to reestablish civilian rule, held elections, but annulled the vote when it disapproved of the results. Instead, an interim civilian government was appointed by the ruling general but it was ousted within a few months by a fourth military coup. Finally, in 1999, civilian rule of sorts was reestablished after years of unrest when former military dictator Olusegun Obasanjo, who had been jailed for criticizing continued military rule, was elected president. President Obasanjo dominated Nigeria for two full presidential terms until the new constitution, which now requires the presidency to alternate between southerners (mostly Christian) and northerners (mostly Muslim), forced him to step aside for a while, beginning with the 2007 election and term of office. Obasanjo's government, however, effectively controlled the result of the 2007 election by illegally removing political rival and Vice-President Atiku Abubakar from election ballots. A last minute Supreme Court intervention put Abubakar's political party, but not his name, back on ballots. But, these last minute ballots had no serial numbers, allowing subsequent ballot stuffing and an election marred by massive fraud. Obasanjo's party colleague, Umaru Yer'Adwa, assumed the presidency. He is widely regarded as a weak stand-in for Obasanjo and the party Obasanjo dominates.

In its first fifty years of independence, then, Nigeria has spent roughly two-thirds of the time under military dictatorship. Even civilian rule has been far from democratic. Apparently, American style constitutions can work even less well elsewhere than they do here. The current Nigerian regime is anything but stable and successful. The country is continually rocked by ethnic and religious violence, massive theft and unparalleled corruption, a huge national debt, dilapidated roads and infrastructure, crippling fuel prices and shortages, organized crime and gang activity, kidnappings, general strikes, a collapsing currency, horrific poverty (70percent live on less than a dollar a day and life expectancy is only 47), and an ongoing AIDS epidemic. There is a growing threat that several mostly Muslim northern states may attempt to secede from the country. These states have adopted religious laws based on the Koran—laws that are restrictive in many ways, especially in denying women education, employment, and public access. Muslim-Christian conflict has mushroomed, Islamic fundamentalism is rapidly growing in popularity, and a second Nigerian civil war may occur soon. Theft and corruption seems to know no bounds. It is generally estimated that roughly ten billion dollars are stolen or wasted every year. The National Assembly has often awarded itself huge bonuses and in-kind benefits. Many of the rural poor try to provide for themselves by breaking into the national oil pipeline (despite shoot-to-kill orders from the army and the constant risk of pipeline explosions that have killed hundreds). The Nigerian bureaucracy is infamously corrupt. Bribes are almost always required to receive government services or even the required forms to merely apply for them. Nigeria's cities feature a few gaudy mansions and massive squalid slums with little in between the two.

All of this has transpired despite the fact that the country has the oil resource to become the second or third largest oil producer in the world. Nigeria is a disappointment; it has failed to come anywhere close to its potential. The country and its people have languished in poverty.

It was in the year of the second military coup and two years before the third one that Achebe wrote his important critique of his country, *The Trouble with Nigeria*. His very brief book poses and answers a basic question: How can a country with so much natural resource and potential constantly end up with such a poor standard of living and such a horrendous quality of life? Ultimately, he answers, the blame falls on unusually large disparities in living standards, rampant corruption, a lack of civic community, and perhaps above all else, the failure of leaders to confront these problems. Achebe describes Nigeria acerbically:

> Nigeria is not a great country. It is one of the most disorderly nations in the world. It is one of the most corrupt, insensitive, inefficient places under the sun. It is one of the most expensive countries and one of those that give the least value for money. It is dirty, callous, noisy, ostentatious, dishonest and vulgar. In short, it is among the most unpleasant places on earth![1]

It often seems to me that the words *corrupt, insensitive, inefficient, dirty, callous, noisy, ostentatious, dishonest,* and *vulgar* resonate loudly in the United States as well as Nigeria. Of course, by third world or African standards, the United States is a marvelous place. But again, the trouble with America is *not* that it is anywhere near the most unpleasant country in the world. The trouble with America is that, despite our unparalleled fortune, America is not among the very best.

The parallels between this book and Achebe's are multifaceted. First and most obvious is the parallel in the main themes. Achebe argues that Nigeria should be one of the most, if not the most, successful countries in Africa, but it is not. I argue here that the United States should be one of the most, if not the most, successful countries in the world. But it is not. Both countries have potential far beyond their current condition.

Second, in both countries it is inadequate political theory that leads to failures of political practice. Patterned on an American model, Nigeria embraced, or at least attempted to embrace, American political beliefs and government structures. Central to both countries is faith in:

- Pluralism (the division of power among many groups and individuals in society) which includes federalism (the division of power between levels of government).
- Constitutionalism (the limitation of government authority and power).
- Capitalism (an economic system in which most of the resource is owned and controlled privately and in which the distribution of income and wealth tends to be highly unequal).

It was the belief of the founders of both countries that pluralism helps prevent the concentration of power, which can invite tyranny; that constitutionalism helps assure the civil liberties of the people by restraining government abuse of them; and that capitalism helps provide a prosperous economy and opportunity for personal advancement.

It is argued here, and to a lesser extent by Achebe in *The Trouble with Nigeria*, that these beliefs are erroneous. Pluralism delivers ineffective and weak government that fails to meet public needs or serve the public will. Constitutionalism restrains the ability of government to do good as well as evil and leaves intact the many threats to freedom that come from non-governmental sources. Capitalism creates massive inequalities that undermine rather than enhance the economic opportunity of most people. Together these three political beliefs and the institutions based upon them constitute the roots of the trouble in both Nigeria and America. Although Nigeria had, and continues to have, ethnic and religious differences and tensions even more intense than those in the United States, it may have been the ineptitude of an American style political system that created the power vacuums that invited the army to take power. In America, it is the ineptitude of our political system that condemns us to bad policies and growing cynicism about our government.

Part I of this book (The Roots of the Trouble) devotes considerable attention to pluralism (chapter 1), constitutionalism (chapter 2), and capitalism (chapter 3) and presents a fairly fundamental critique of American political theory and practice. In other words, it is not just the current leaders and policies of America that are inadequate, it is the basic institutions, principles, and political theory upon which they are based and via which they are assured. America has poor leaders and bad policy *because* its basic institutions, founding principles, and political theory are fatally flawed.

In America, our limitations upon government come in many forms. Pluralism restrains government by pitting us all against one another (leader against leader, government branch against government branch, interest group against interest group, individual against individual). Actually, it is more complex than that. Pluralism is a system of intense and extensive checks and balances that cut across every aspect of American government and society. Everyone is pitted against everyone else so that no group or individual can have enough power to tyrannize the rest. Constitionalism restrains government by limiting the legal scope of its authority and by creating institutional practices, such as the court system's power of judicial review, to help assure that government power is in fact, as well as theory, constrained. Capitalism restrains government by anointing wealthy private individuals, not government or society collectively, as the principal owners and controllers of most of the economy. All of these institutional foundations are intended to assure that our government cannot tyrannize us.

Of course, what we Americans generally fail to see is that this also tends to assure that our government is too weak to help us. One of the major themes of this book is that a government too weak to help us is also too weak to represent us. Even more important than our faith in pluralism, constitutionalism, and capitalism is our American belief in the need for representative government. And yet we fail to see that there is a contradiction between pluralism, constitutionalism, and capitalism on the one hand and representative government on the other hand. When government is constrained, it is the will of the people that government represents that is also constrained.

Another parallel between *The Trouble with Nigeria* and this book is stylistic. Achebe's book is a polemic (in other words, an impassioned partisan argument, not the neutral or objective discussion found in most textbooks). Like most polemics, it is brief and to the point. In fact, it is little more than a pamphlet. This book is also polemical and in it I strive to be concise. Although this is a much larger and more systematic analysis than Achebe's book provides, I do not intend to mince words or pull any punches. In this book, I will argue that the problems of America are embedded into the very principles of government built into our constitution and society, and unquestioned by almost every American. It is my hope that this book will encourage readers to think more critically about what they think they know about American government and politics.

There are also other themes found in both Achebe's book and this one. Achebe is very critical of extreme inequalities in income and wealth and of government policies that exacerbate them. So am I. Achebe criticizes localism (loyalties to one's ethnicity, town, city, or state that he believes undermine support for the country as a whole). I do, too. Achebe does not have much confidence in the political leaders of his county. I don't have high regard for the leaders of my country, either.

Several of the sections in this book are partially patterned on ones found in *The Trouble with Nigeria*. Achebe's first chapter is entitled "Where the Problem Lies." This introduction, you may recall, is entitled "Where the Trouble Lies." Achebe's third chapter is entitled "False Image of Ourselves." I make reference to that phrase in a section of chapter 4, "Making a Mess of

Things at Home: The American Domestic Policy Environment." Paralleling Achebe, I critique American political culture as distressingly self-absorbed and ungenerous. I also borrow from the title of his fourth chapter, "Leadership, Nigerian-Style" in my critique of American politicians, "Leadership, American-Style," another section of chapter 4. Beyond that, the organization and content of this book is fairly unique and is in no way attributable to Mr. Achebe. America, after all, is not Nigeria and our troubles are, in many ways, unique and complex.

In short, despite many parallels and the obvious inspiration that Achebe provided for this text, this book does stand on its own. The flaws of American government and society are serious and troubling in their implications. America may look elsewhere in the world for clues about alternatives to its current course, but I doubt if many of those clues will emanate from Nigeria. America's political theory, government, and economy have profoundly influenced Nigeria—for the worse, I suspect—but Nigeria has not significantly influenced the United States. The trouble with America is of our own making and the solutions to our problems are likely to remain our own responsibility. This book is written with the assumption that we need to do more to acknowledge the inadequacies of our own political system, certainly to better understand it and hopefully, at some point, to begin to find ways to significantly change it for the better.

Part II of this book offers close examination of many of the details concerning the inadequacies of American politics and policies. Included in chapter 4 are the following sections critiquing American domestic policy:

- The Reverse Robin Hood: A critique of political and economic policies that create huge inequalities in income and wealth, impose unfair and regressive taxation, and develop inequalities in the distributions of costs and opportunities.
- The New Tribalism: We tend to use the word "tribe" in a rather racist way to refer to groups we perceive as primitive (such as Native American, Africans, Asian Islanders, etc.) but strictly speaking a tribe is an ethnic group and tribalism is, as Achebe claims, "discrimination against a citizen because of his place of birth."[2] In America, we have a new form of tribalism, our own version of loyalty to one's own race or ethnicity, or to one's own home community or state: localism and federalism. Racism is critiqued in this book as an inexorable and fundamental reality in America. Localism and federalism are interpreted as a means of weakening government and of allowing privileged groups to evade taxes and thwart change.
- Political Culture: American political culture is seen as collectively self-absorbed, greedy, uncaring, irresponsible, and ungenerous even though individually we are fairly affable, friendly, practical, and tolerant.

- Leadership, American Style: Our politicians are described as non-leaders who undermine our representation and cater to our worst impulses.
- The New Anarchy: A critique of the growing American tendency to want smaller, less ambitious, and much cheaper government, even though our need for good government and ambitious policy is growing exponentially.

Included in chapter 5, "A Menace to the World: The American Foreign Policy Environment," are these two sections critiquing American foreign policy:

- War Mongering: As much as American government has been restrained domestically, it has been hyperactive and malevolent in its foreign policy. To the rest of the world, the United States is a source of violence and instability that actively undermines, rather than enhances, the cause of democracy.
- The New Imperialism: The United States has become a global empire that enriches our economy, and especially the wealthiest of Americans, at the great expense of most of the third world.

Taken together, part II suggests that American government is far from the best anywhere.

Some readers might object that, if I find American government and society so fundamentally flawed, I should leave the country. Many of the protesters, critics, and reformers of the 1960s were confronted with counter demonstrators shouting "Love it or leave it." That slogan seems predicated on a false assumption. Strange as it may seem to some, I do love this country. Harsh criticisms of the sort found here are not the opposite of love. Ask any spouse, parent, or child: *indifference*, not criticism, is the opposite of love. If someone doesn't care what you do, she or he doesn't love you. If someone bothers to offer criticism (especially if it is constructive criticism and not mere name-calling), then at least you know he or she cares enough to take an interest. In this book, I attempt to offer constructive criticism. Because this book offers perspectives not typically found in textbooks on American government and politics, I hope that it can promote more critical thinking by readers. I do *not* expect that this book will enhance the chances of reformers and activists in any efforts to overhaul our political system. If I am correct that our political system is hyper-resistant even to small significant changes, then a fundamental political reform of our system is exceedingly unlikely anytime soon. However, ours is a system that does not work well and it may, at some juncture, simply collapse from the weight of political problems that eventually culminate in crises. In a brief Postscript, "Is America Reparable?" I briefly offer some suggestions as to what it means to speak up for what is right and some speculation about the hope for a better America someday.

Chinua Achebe also addressed the love it or leave it issue in his polemic. His answer is somewhat similar. He wrote his book because Nigeria is not completely beyond redemption. He stays in Nigeria because it is where God put him; it is his homeland. He hopes to be part of the process of improving it because, in his own way, he loves his country and its people. He concludes, "Nigerians are what they are only because their leaders are *not* what *they* should be."[3] My conclusion is somewhat different: we Americans (including our leaders) are not all that we should be, only because our political system is *not* what *it* should be.

NOTES

1. Chinua Achebe, *The Trouble with Nigeria* (London: Heinemann, 1984), 9–10.
2. Chinua Achebe, *Trouble*, 7.
3. Chinua Achebe, *Trouble*, 10.

Part I

THE ROOTS OF THE TROUBLE

1

Pluralism and Its Discontents

Either the existence of the same passion or interest in a majority at the same time, must be prevented; or the majority, having such co-existent passion or interest, must be rendered, by their number and local situation, unable to concert and carry into effect schemes of oppression.

—James Madison, *Federalist Number 10*[1]

The strategy of *Federalist No. 10* is to divide and make politically impotent; it does and we are.

—David F. Schuman, *A Preface to Politics*[2]

The most significant fact about the distribution of power in America is not who makes such decisions as are made, but rather how many matters of the greatest social importance are not objects of anyone's decision at all.

—Robert Paul Wolff, *The Poverty of Liberalism*[3]

In terms of generating policy solutions to our common public problems, the American political system is working exactly as it was intended to work—poorly. Our political system was *not* created to make policy formation or government efficacy easy or likely. Its central goal was to help us avoid tyranny, to make it impossible for any group—even the majority of the population—to amass enough power to abuse everyone else. It does accomplish this, but it does so at a terrible cost.

Pluralism can be defined as the division of power among many groups and individuals in government and society.[4] It lies at the very heart of all of our

3

political structures. It is at once the means of avoiding the nightmare of tyranny and the obstacle to the achievement of almost all our other collective needs and wants. In short, the gridlock, the fragmentation, the radical decentralization, the power vacuums, the political infighting, the ineptitude, the wastefulness, and ultimately the impotence of government in America are all here *not* by error but by design. They are all part and parcel of a grand plan to prevent tyranny. The plan works well and, as a result, our government doesn't. Almost all of the problems which plague American government are, in some way, attributable to the pluralistic structures constitutionally sewn into our political institutions by design, based on the flawed political reasoning of our founders.

The circumstances of the emergence of a pluralist constitution in America are well known, but often students of politics come away from the story of our founding marveling at the brilliant creativity of our founding fathers and dangerously oblivious to the tragic and ongoing implications of their imaginative "solutions." Let us briefly review the story of our political founding yet again, but this time from a far more critical perspective.

American revolutionaries of course resisted the unfairness of taxation, and high taxation at that, without representation. Of course, of taxation and the lack of representation, what really ticked off most colonists was the taxation! Had Britain offered the American colonists representation in Parliament, the number of Americans was probably not large enough to vote down the taxes and a revolution may have ensued anyway. In a way, the American Revolution was the first in a long series of taxpayer revolts in this country. With that being our major objective, the American Revolution was a fairly conservative Revolution, at least when compared with those revolutions (e.g., the French revolution a few years later) that sought to change the whole social order and not primarily the tax codes.

Our earliest independent government, under the Articles of Confederation, was hardly a government at all. All thirteen states had to agree before any national law could be enacted. Because this hardly ever happened, the thirteen states were fairly autonomous and this is almost certainly what most Americans wanted. Our grade school students are still taught that this was problematic because different states had different currencies, because of the intensity of interstate commercial conflict, and because criminals could avoid prosecution by crossing state lines. Of course, significant problems did eventually arise but these were not them. Changing currency was not an enormous ordeal, getting from one state to the next was! A far smaller proportion of people traveled between states at that time than travel between countries now. Quite frankly, there was not a big interstate commercial problem because there was not a lot of interstate travel, let alone interstate commerce (the only major exception being the Chesapeake Bay region where interstate commerce could be achieved without overland travel). A negligible number of the relatively fewer criminals around back then dared to attempt escape via interstate travel. It was far too arduous and dangerous. Their chances of not getting caught by staying home were much better.

The real problems with the Articles of Confederation were apparent by the mid-1780s, about a decade after the onset of the American Revolution at Lexington and Concord (1775) and within a few years of the formal British capitulation to American independence in 1783. Warfare gave way to economic depression. The depression was due not just to the ravages of war itself, but also to a massive debt incurred by borrowing huge amounts from the various enemies of Britain (especially France) to buy weapons and other supplies needed to secure victory. Making the economy even worse and further isolating the new country from the international economy, with one state or another buckling under the stress of depression, the confederation could not agree to make payments on the national debt because the Articles required unanimity. Rhode Island, an odd state dominated by the political clout of debtors rather than creditors, introduced paper currency much to the shock of other states and creditors everywhere. This allowed debtors to make payments in cheap currency that wasn't really worth its face value and wasn't equivalent to debts that had been incurred.

Sadly, our founders thought that those innovations (like paper currency) that favored the poor amounted to theft from the rich, but they had little problem with the more common practices that made them rich at the expense of the poor. Even more distressing to them was the shock of Shays' Rebellion in western Massachusetts. On the verge of going to debtors prison due to inability to pay the increased state taxes, revolutionary war Captain Daniel Shays led many of his compatriots from town to town in a rampage that burned down courthouses and town halls to block foreclosure proceedings against poor farmers. Although a *privately* assembled militia eventually dispersed the rebels, neither the national Congress nor Massachusetts were able to raise a *public* militia to do so. The question of the day was this: would the American Revolution prove to be a mere prelude to a second taxpayer revolution, one that promised to be more violent and certainly more intra-American than the first?

The political problem became quite obvious. Americans needed to revamp their national government to enable it to have the power to:

- make payments on the debt (needed to improve the economy)
- prevent "irresponsible" states from catering to the mob by introducing paper money, abolishing debts, or imposing equal divisions of property

- prevent populist rebellions from subverting first localities, then a state, and eventually the nation itself

At the same time, how could all this be accomplished without making this newly empowered national government itself a threat to our liberty? After all, what good is it to prevent tyranny from emerging from the grassroots of society and taking over from below, if instead society seems likely to be subverted and tyrannized from the top down by national government officials themselves? Ultimately, our founders had an imaginative answer to their particular historical predicament but, unfortunately, we're still paying the price for their creative "solution"—pluralism—today.

Nowhere do we find a more succinct and more articulate explanation of our founders' "solution" and the reasoning that went into it, than in James Madison's "Federalist Paper Number 10." Madison, of course, was one of the most influential of our founders, generally regarded as the "father of the U.S. Constitution." *The Federalist Papers* are brief articles (editorials really) that appeared, anonymously authored, in a New York City newspaper in 1787 and 1788 to persuade citizens in New York to support the proposed Constitution's ratification in that pivotally important state. Madison is now known to be the author of "Federalist Number 10," generally regarded as the best of these papers, and he is remarkably candid and clear in his discussion of the central purpose and intent of the U.S. Constitution and the logic that went into its creation.

Madison's argument is built on an explicitly negative view of human nature. According to Madison, we humans are *by nature* selfish and competitive. We are, by nature, predisposed to mutual animosity. We are more inclined to vex and oppress each other than to cooperate for our common good. We also possess a zeal for different and incompatible opinions on every topic, especially religion and politics. According to Madison, we are *not* particularly reasonable or logical. We are quick to form attachments to all sorts of political leaders who find it fairly easy to get us to run off and support efforts that might very well be in their interest but run counter to our own best interest. In short, human nature makes us both selfish and a bit stupid and our stupidity can frequently undermine our ability to be successfully selfish. The violence of our conflicts of opinion is fueled by meaningful differences in economic interest (for example, the differences between rich and poor, creditors and debtors, manufacturers and plantation owners, and so on). Nonetheless, our nature is so contrary, says Madison, that we are likely to become embroiled in conflicts over even the "most frivolous and fanciful" differences between us.

Based on this view of human nature, Madison's "Federalist Number 10" argues that the central problem of government, at any time or place, is faction. Although no longer an everyday word, "faction" refers to any group of people who come together to pursue a common interest or passion, which is incompatible with the common good. Political parties and interest groups are formal examples of factions. But most factions are probably informal and occur wherever people conspire to advance their group's interest to the detriment of others. What makes factions so problematic is that our very nature, in Madison's estimation, guarantees that we will all often conspire with others to pursue common interests or passions that will undermine the common good. In short, we all engage in a multitude and diversity of factious behaviors. We seldom ask what we can do that is genuinely good for our whole country. Instead, we typically run off, sometimes half-cocked, based on various notions, often false, about what we can do for ourselves. Of course, factions come in all sizes and strengths but Madison was particularly concerned about factions that constitute a majority of the whole population because they would seem to be the hardest to contain.

In "Federalist Paper Number 10," Madison asks if we can eliminate the causes of faction. We could abolish liberty. But what would happen if we promised to kill or even torture individuals we caught engaged in factious behavior? The long and violent history of political dictatorships would seem to suggest that this strategy can be fairly effective. Madison agreed but he rejected this "solution" anyway on the grounds that it was worse than the disease of faction itself. In his famous analogy, he argued that eliminating air puts out fire but also kills off animal life. Eliminating liberty cuts way back on factious behavior but it also kills decent political life (that is, freedom and representative government). Madison also argued that it was impossible to eliminate faction by giving everyone the same opinion about everything. As long as people have imperfect reason and the freedom to act upon it, they will form incompatible opinions (and groups). Of course, Madison was obviously writing well before the era of television and mass communication, the influence of which will be discussed in chapter 2. Suffice it to say for now, mass media can be a powerful tool for the allocation of at least some opinions. Still, Madison was certainly right that we cannot allocate to everyone the same opinions about everything. Even if we could, it would raise the same troubling questions by undermining genuine freedom and rendering representation a mere farce.

Instead, Madison's "solution" to his problem with faction lies elsewhere: in controlling its effects. In other words, we will learn to live with the problem by minimizing the harm that it causes. But before considering that "solution," it is important not to lose sight of just what the basic theoretical problem is here. Our entire political system is based on this Madisonian notion that we can and should have representative government in spite of the fact that the people are neither virtuous nor trustworthy. Early advocates of representative government had to work hard to argue that commoners were capable of playing some role in self-rule (i.e., that they were smart enough, responsible enough, and, yes, virtuous enough to participate in their own governance). The prevailing political arguments held that aristocrats alone had training to minimize the effects of negative human nature (in other words, becoming virtuous is very difficult and only those who have enough wealth to enable them to focus most of their efforts on attaining virtue, aristocrats, were likely to have much success). Representative government could only be possible if the bulk of the population could be virtuous. Indeed, throughout the American Revolution, our founders subscribed to Radical Whig ideology, which held that popular government is only possible if virtually all are good. Later on, after troubles such as Shays' Rebellion, it became difficult to view Americans as homogeneous, harmonious, *or* virtuous. As a political theorist, what may be most novel about Madison is his development of ideas about using popular government to contain people and not just to represent them. Clearly, Madison is among the first *advocates* of representative government to argue that the people can be tyrants and that tyranny of a majority may be one of the most difficult types of tyranny to overcome.

One of the most amazing things about American political institutions is that they are based on some remarkably pessimistic views of humanity. Perhaps this is not surprising. Ours is one of the oldest representative governments in the world. It is based on some *relatively* ancient (18th century) and snobbish notions about human nature and virtue. As we will see later, many representative governments with more contemporary origins are based on considerably less classist and snobbish notions about virtue, and much more optimistic assumptions about the ability of the majority to wield political power responsibly. By contrast, however, the American political system seems be based on the unwritten motto: representative government *in spite of the people.*

It is no wonder that Madison and our other founding fathers did not like the word *democracy.* They were advocates of a republic, not a democracy. In their view, democracies entrust unfettered power in the hands of the majority, thus inviting abuse of the minority and violent political instability. Nowadays, we Americans describe our government as democratic all the time but we probably shouldn't. Based on its ancient Greek roots the word democracy literally means the many (or the people) rule. It may be argued that a pure democracy can only exist where the people directly govern themselves and not where schemes of representation are employed as the next best practical alternative to direct self-rule. By this standard, there may have been no democracy in the history of the planet. The occasional "pure democracies" of ancient Athens excluded most of the population (the poor, slaves, women) as non-citizens. The all-town meetings of some New England communities exercise merely local authority when more significant decisions are made representationally instead at the state and national level. But, I am not such a purist. The term democracy seems to me perfectly well suited to any society that entrusts the majority with political power. But that is most decidedly *not* the United States. Instead, Madison's republican remedy to the problem of faction, so articulately revealed in "Federalist Paper Number 10," entrusts no one with political power. Our political system pits everyone against everyone else so that everyone, including the majority, will be contained.

This strategy of contently pitting everyone against everyone else in a myriad of ways is, in a word, pluralism. Madison called it "the republican remedy" to the problem of faction. Notice his use of the term republican rather than democratic. Republic literally means "the public thing" and the implication of the word is that the political realm belongs to the people rather than to some monarch or aristocratic class. But ownership of the realm alone does *not* imply, as democracy does, the right of the people, or the majority, to exercise day-to-day control of political decision making. Here then are the highlights of his "republican remedy" as described to us in "Federalist Paper Number 10":

- Separation of Powers: Divide government against itself by structuring the institutions in such a way that the people influencing executive, legislative, and judicial functions are less likely to commingle and cooperate as much as they might otherwise (in other words, create three basic branches of government to encourage each one to try to thwart the other two).
- Checks and Balances: Give the three basic branches of American government specific powers designed to help assure their success in limiting the power of the other two branches. For example, a President can contain the legislature with veto power and can contain the courts by withholding enforcement of judicial rulings or by manipulating them via judicial appointment recommendations. The legislature can contain the executive by withholding funding and can contain the courts by withholding funds for enforcing judicial rulings or via its judicial appointment confirmation powers. The judiciary can contain the executive or the legislature the same way, via judicial review (striking down their actions by interpreting them as violations of the U.S. Constitution). These are just the highlights of our checks and balances, a *Reader's Digest* version if you will. The checks and balances of the American political system are as diverse and intense as they are ubiquitous.
- Bicameralism: Because the legislature is traditionally regarded as the branch of popular government closest to, and most responsive to, the people, divide it into two competing houses. Give each house different constituencies, different terms of office, and different powers and

procedures to help guarantee conflict between them. No, American bicameralism was not a mere byproduct of the need to resolve differences in concepts of representation. The Connecticut Compromise was not so much aimed at compromising between the New Jersey and Virginia Plans as it was aimed at compromising the power of Congress itself. Look at what Madison had to say about this in his "Federalist Paper Number 51": "In republican government the legislative authority, necessarily, predominates. The remedy for this inconveniency is, to divide the legislature into different branches; and to render them by different modes of election, and different principles of action, as little connected with each other, as the nature of their common functions, and their common dependence on society, will admit."[5]

- Indirect Government: Do not let the people exercise unlimited direct control of the process of electing public officials. For example, in presidential elections, voters still elect only the electors who, in turn, select a president and vice-president. The influence of the voters is indirect and filtered. Presidential electors are free to exercise their judgement even if it means subverting voter preference. Our original means of electing U.S. Senators was likewise indirect. Voters elected state legislators and state legislators appointed the U.S. Senators for their state. The idea is that the people, left unchecked or unfiltered, might themselves be a source of tyranny.

- Federalism: Divide power between levels of government. Reserve some powers for the states and other powers for the national government so that each level of government can check and balance (that is, obstruct) the other level. Of course, just as there is simultaneous competition and mutual obstruction within the national level (for example, among the three major branches), so too it is expected and desired that there will be checks and balances among the states as they compete against *each other* for resource and influence (and in the process help deny one another both).

- Dual Sovereignty: Create what Madison called a "mixed" or "compound" republic wherein in some regards the political system seems to assume that the people are sovereign (in other words, have the right to direct government) but in other regards it assumes that the states are sovereign. For example, the equal representation of states in the Senate makes sense only if the states are sovereign. On the other hand, the representation based on population size characteristic of the House makes sense only if the people are sovereign. Make both assumptions simultaneously to help fortify the checks and balances to be found in bicameralism and federalism. This also encourages the ambiguity that fuels intense conflicts (for example, the Civil War) over the meaning and scope of "states rights."

In short, this "republican remedy" is nothing other than an *institutionalized* pluralism. The distribution of power among many groups and individuals in government and society is guaranteed by a structure of institutions that is constantly pitting everyone against everyone else for the express purpose of preventing anyone (and everyone) from becoming particularly powerful.

But this list of constitutional features does not do justice to the scope of American pluralism. Pluralism is not limited to our governmental structures or the relationship between them. It pervades the entire society. It is by design that the United States has an enormous array of interest groups, all lobbying, contributing, letter writing, picketing, or even bringing lawsuits to try to pull American government in a particular direction. Actually, they are trying to pull American government in mutually incompatible directions and America doesn't go very far in *any* direction as a result. The stuff of American pluralism is the competition *between* factions. This is even more prevalent outside the halls of government than it is within them. In short, Madison's remedy uses "ambition against ambition." Based on his shrewd theory, our political society encourages us all to be factious so that the *effects* of faction will be minimized. We cancel each other out. Or, as Schuman put it, we are divided against each other and, in the process, made impotent.

There is nothing particularly new about this strategy. Years before *The Federalist Papers*, in 1776, British economist Adam Smith argued that public virtue *can* come out of private vice. Smith was a far more nuanced thinker than many economic conservatives acknowledge, especially those who profess to admire him most.[6] Smith's famous book, *The Wealth of Nations*, is widely interpreted by such conservatives in ways that support the assertion that everyone should simply be as self-interested and competitive as possible. If we all did this and government left us alone to do so (rather than foolishly and dangerously trying to regulate the economy), everyone in society would prosper more than they would otherwise, even those with the least talent, industry, or luck. Just by trying to be greedy, the argument supposedly goes, we actually can do more good than if we are trying to be charitable or helpful. Public virtue (making society and the people in it more prosperous) ironically emanates from private vice (being as greedy as you can manage). This is exactly what Madison was saying, only he, Madison, applies it to politics rather than economics. Everyone should be as politically ambitious and selfish as possible. If we do this, all ambition and selfishness will be contained by other ambition and selfishness and we will never know tyranny. Of course, Smith was wrong as well as a bit misinterpreted.[7] Even by 1776, the rich in Britain were getting richer at the expense of those who were poorer. And, as we will see, Madison may be wrong too. Perhaps our system saves us from tyranny but it simultaneously condemns us to our ongoing problems and robs us of democracy.

In some countries, pluralism is merely a cultural phenomenon. In other words, a culture may be diverse because there is great variety in social class, economic interest, race and ethnicity, religion, ideology, etc. Often when this is the case, a representative government ends up with broadly dispersed power precisely because it is representative of the people and their lack of consensus. In the United States, we also have plenty of *cultural* pluralism (because we have so little consensus) but what distinguishes our government from saner varieties of representational politics is this *institutional* pluralism, which is the very soul of Madison's "republican remedy." The far-flung distribution of checks and balances guarantees a broad distribution of power. Our political system seems intent on perpetuating gridlock. This is not happenstance. Madison did not fear that we would fail to reach majority agreements. He was afraid that we might succeed in reaching them. And, so, our political system is designed to resist the "encroachments" of even the majority.

So who exactly is this "majority faction" that Madison so feared? What group, constituting a majority of the population, could be conspiring to pursue a common interest or passion contrary to the good of the whole society? Women? No, Madison's era did not quite consider women to be fully human. Women had no rights to vote or hold office and wielded negligible political power. Similarly, non-whites and the property*less* had no suffrage rights at this primitive point in time. However, Madison did have reason to worry about the potential clout of the propertied *poor*, those who could perhaps just modestly exceed the property qualifications for voting but were far more numerous than the propertied rich. This was the majority that might sympathize with the likes of Daniel Shays, have a desire for paper money, and lobby for an abolition of debts or a more equal distribution of property. All of these things were of great potential appeal to the majority and they were all viewed by Madison and his peers as "improper and wicked projects."

And, so, we have a political system that is designed to make change difficult and which requires far more than majority support before a political change can be achieved. Obviously, ours is a political system that can generally create and sustain change only when there is a confluence of support for it among the three basic branches of government. At the national level, for example, Congress must pass a law, a president must sign it (or at least fail to veto it), and the courts must not strike it down as unconstitutional. If any of these three things fail to happen, the hope for change is basically dead. Yes, occasionally Congress may override a veto but this happens only one or two percent of the time at best. Presidents do make policy via executive order without Congressional action but this is not where sweeping or substantive policy changes can emerge. Put simply, all budget bills must originate in the House of Representatives and not much significant new policy can develop without the money with which to make it possible.

But here we are just scratching the surface of the American political system's resistance to change. Support for change, *any* change, by any one of the three branches of government, itself requires an amazing confluence of effort before it can emerge. For example, Congress can pass a law only if a bill survives a complex trek through myriad committees and subcommittees by winning each and every vote at each and every juncture. These junctures may easily amount to a dozen, two dozen, or even more votes in the House of Representatives. Congressional committees generally separate their consideration of the bill's two basic aspects: its concept (authorization) and its funding (appropriations). If a bill wins authorization in one set of committees, but is denied appropriations by another set of committees, or vice versa, it is defeated. Hostile special interest groups may plan to organize their efforts to defeat the bill around one or two committees or subcommittees where the political composition suggests the bill is most vulnerable. Those who oppose change have only to win once to defeat change whereas supporters of change have to win over and over and over yet again to prevail.

And the price of success, when it does occur, is political compromise that generally dilutes the meaningfulness and effectiveness of the legislation. If a bill does make it through the House, it must repeat its Homeric success in the Senate before any real accomplishment is possible. If the Senate fails to pass the bill in absolutely identical form, the bill is dead. Majority support (either from the American people themselves or from members of Congress) is not enough to assure passage for several reasons. First, in order for a bill to have majority support within all the committee and subcommittee votes along the way, there needs to be at least a bit more than simple majority support in the chamber as a whole. For example, if a bill is supported by only 223 of 445 members of the House, there may be no way to deliver a majority supporting a bill across all the committee and subcommittee votes. If the majority party's leadership strongly favors the bill, it may choose to work with the Rules Committee to abridge the normal committee process in hope of passing the bill. But this simply means that, on some occasions, Congressional leaders may facilitate change rather than act more typically by burying it. In any event, 223 supporters in the House can only be enough to assure passage if the 223 includes pivotal majority leaders and a fortunate majority within the Rules Committee.

The Senate, being a much smaller body, is much less influenced by its committee system. Yet, it has its own quirks that impair change. Senate debate rules allow unlimited speaking time. A minority opposing change may defeat a clear-cut majority supporting it by engaging in a filibuster (i.e., simply refusing to stop talking until the bill is withdrawn from consideration).

Senate rules that provide for cloture (cutting off debate and calling the question) require 60 votes for passage. Thus, in the U.S. Senate, 41 opponents of a bill can easily defeat 59 proponents of it. And, of course, Senators having a statewide constituency and much longer term of office are, by Madison's design, predisposed to disagree with their House colleagues. Historically, the centrist Senate tends to be more moderate than the House of Representatives, which tends to be more ideologically partisan (relatively conservative when there is a Republican majority and relatively liberal when there is a Democratic majority).

Consequently, it should not be surprising that relatively little legislation survives the gauntlet that is Congress. In the typical Congressional (two-year) term, about 10,000 bills and resolutions are introduced. Far less than 10 percent reach the floor of either house for any action (for example, a vote, amendment, or referral back to committee). Generally, each two-year term, only about 400 bills are passed and, of those, only half are of any significance (that is, are the subject of hearings or debate or receive media coverage). The other half do such things as create honorary naming of buildings or days, offer commendations or citations, authorize honorary coins, stamps, or monuments, etc. Consequently, if a President vetoes just ten bills a year, he or she may be wiping out a tenth or more of Congress's significant legislation.

The biggest obstacle to change in America is not the pluralism between branches of government, but rather the pluralism within them. However, if you dislike change, you may love American politics. In a sense, our political system favors conservatives over reformers because change is so difficult to achieve. But there are times when American conservative ideology calls for changes too (for example, lowering taxes, restructuring the tax system, augmenting police powers, or restricting abortion). Here, "conservative" ideologues are as likely to be frustrated and defeated as the most liberal reformer. Our political system makes difficult changes of any sort or of any direction. And the price of any "success" is very likely to be compromise. There are many Political Scientists, as well as politicians and everyday citizens, who seem to like it this way. Those who ascribe to the pluralist theory of American government not only acknowledge that in America power is widely divided, but also assert that this is a very good thing. After all, it does prevent tyranny and compromise seems a good thing to all that are greatly worried about the rights of the minority. Virtually every group has at least some say and gets at least a little bit of what they want (including not having to accept what they consider unacceptable). Isn't this desirable? Political Scientist David Truman is well known for having gone so far as to suggest that the American national interest is nothing other than the sum total of private group and self-interests. Furthermore, if these interests do largely cancel each other out, that itself may be described as providing us with our fair share at least in a society that places more of an emphasis on avoiding the unpleasant than achieving the pleasant.

In other words, our fair share as a partisan of one ideology may be not having to put up with political policies dictated by partisans of another ideology. Maybe one hundred heavily compromised federal laws per year are all we really want or need. There are those who think so, but I keep thinking about how the condition of our people compares unfavorably with the condition of people in other representative governments (in health, education, security, economic mobility, etc.). If we really do just want to be left alone for the most part, I'm not sure it is a particularly rational desire.

Nonetheless, American pluralist theory endorses Madison's theory of government and politics. In essence, its advocates argue that, in America, power is genuinely divided among many groups and interests and that this is precisely as it should be. Pluralist theory arose out of the ashes of the traditional democratic theory of American government, which dominated the early history of the discipline of Political Science. Formally stated, traditional democratic theory held that, in America, public decisions are mediated through the bulk of the population. In other words, it claimed that we have an informed and active citizenry that holds politicians accountable to serving the people's wants and needs. From this view, politicians were seen as incapable of drifting very far from the ever present, well-defined will of their constituents. Citizens were viewed by this dated theory as generally equal in influence, thus rendering the will of the majority as decisive in controlling the direction of American government and politics.

Even by the middle of the twentieth century, Political Scientists had sufficiently surveyed the sorry state of the American citizenry's level of political knowledge and activity to realize that this theory was no longer viable. For example, most Americans cannot name their own Congressional representatives, let alone have a good idea of what policies they pursue. Only a minority of Americans have an accurate idea as to what the general differences are between liberals and conservatives. Relatively few Americans engage in any political activities beyond voting (e.g., letter writing, protesting, lobbying, making political contributions, etc.) and about half the population doesn't even bother to vote.

Pluralist theory evolved out of an attempt to revise the obviously inaccurate traditional democratic theory. Perhaps most closely associated with the work of Robert Dahl and his famous *Who Governs?* study of the distribution of power in New Haven, Connecticut,[8] pluralist theory emerged contending that groups, not individuals, were the firebrands of the American political process. Most individuals may be uninformed and passive, but for nearly every conceivable individual and interest, there is at least one (and typically far more than one) group that is informed and active advocating on behalf of those individuals and interests. In Dahl's reading, then, the people are still basically sovereign even though most may be anything but politically aware or savvy, suggesting that there is a plurality of competing groups (and interests) such that no single group (or interest) could ever possess anything approaching a majority of power let alone a monopoly of control. Madison is seen as having achieved exactly what he was hoping to attain: a dispersal or scattering of power in the United States with constant competition between groups, no group in control, and no group completely without voice.

The unwritten motto of American government from pluralist theory's perspective may not be "One person, one vote," but perhaps instead "Every group its share." Neither power nor wealth is distributed equally, but these inequalities are viewed by pluralists as legitimate if no one has all or a majority of power and no one is completely powerless. Representative government is seen as achieved even though the ignorance and passivity of so many people may not make it as easy or simple as it is described in traditional democratic theory. If these competing groups often cancel each other out so that no policy ensues or if policy innovation can occur only when competing groups are willing to compromise with one another and settle for a little bit of their agenda of preference, there is no problem. Pluralist theorists claim that under America's reasonable rules of governance, compromise and refusal to proceed in the absence of relative consensus are the hallmarks of representation.

Nonetheless, pluralists are remarkably optimistic about the possibility that disparate groups with divergent wants and needs can come together and work out their differences well enough to build policy by developing a complex web of alliances and compromises all along the way. In 1949, prominent pluralist civil service scholar, Paul Appleby, referred to this remarkable phenomenon as "mesh,"[9] prompting some critics to respond that it is instead "mush." Clearly, American government does manage to generate some policy. As we saw above, at the national level, about 200 policy related laws are enacted each year. Perhaps what best determines one's opinion of pluralist theory is one's opinion of the laws that American government generates. If it is coherent, effective legislation that genuinely helps us solve our most pressing public problems, perhaps it is "mesh" after all. However, much of the remainder of this book will assert that careful examination of what our government does and does not achieve, as compared to other representative governments, suggests that ultimately our government yields "mush."

Pluralist theory seems to invest a great deal in the argument that myriad and meaningful compromises are not only possible but also desirable. They simultaneously help prevent any group from getting far too much at the expense of others and they help prevent pure stagnation. And, at least conceptually, compromise does offer a practical approach to resolving impasses. For example, if the idea of a large tax cut is in dispute, a compromise result may be a small or moderate size tax cut. If the idea of building a new superhighway is in dispute, a compromise outcome may be constructing a smaller or less costly version of the project. There are some things (especially material goods or services) that just seem particularly well suited to compromise and there are many who seem to believe that compromise is the essence of fairness. After all, even small children are encouraged to take turns or to take some disputed object, let's say a candy bar, and cut it into equal pieces for all to share. Of course, in American pluralist politics, we hardly end up with equal pieces. Perhaps most everyone ends up with at least something, but some people get enormously more than others do.

In addition, there are those issues that are not particularly well suited to compromise—for example, moral issues. How do you satisfactorily compromise morality? Consider, for example, the abortion issue. To pro-life partisans, abortion constitutes homicide, is *not* a morally permissible choice, and should *not* be legal with the possible exception of when the mother's life is placed in genuine jeopardy by the pregnancy (i.e., when *another* life is likely to be ended). To most pro-choice partisans, abortion does *not* constitute homicide, *is* a morally permissible choice, and the lives of women should *not* be devastated by the imposition of unwanted pregnancies (and children). In general, this is an issue that seems to hinge on the question of whether what the pro-life call an unborn baby and the pro-choice call a fetus, constitutes a person and, if so, at what point. There are some pro-choice advocates who navigate this troublesome issue somewhat uniquely. They may acknowledge the personhood of the fetus, but nonetheless argue that unwanted pregnancies can be deadly for would-be mothers in ways far beyond physical dangers of gestation and delivery. Unwanted pregnancy can cause such ostracism as to lead to the new mother's murder, suicide, or such impaired life circumstances as to cause grossly premature death in any of a wide variety of ways (not the least of which are associated with poverty).

What compromise can make everyone satisfied here? It is unimaginable because the basic questions are moral in nature and morality quickly loses it meaning and integrity when it is compromised. Nonetheless, our pluralist political system imposes compromises even on issues that are essentially moral in nature. In the case of abortion, our current policy, based on a pro-choice victory in Roe v. Wade, renders first trimester abortions *legally* permissible. The implication of this portion of our policy would seem to be that first trimester abortions are *morally* permissible. On the other hand, the pro-life victory in passing the Hyde Amendment (constitutionally sustained in Harris v. McRae) denies public funding for women who want an abortion but cannot afford one. (Advocates of the Hyde Amendment are well aware that the government spends hundreds times more on benefits to unwanted children than it would have spent on abortions, but the reason for supporting the amendment is based on moral, not economic, reasoning.) In many cases, the costs of abortion include not only the fees for the procedure, but, given the controversy, terror, and violence which surround this issue, the personal and economic costs of traveling hundreds of miles to find the nearest provider. Other laws upheld by the Supreme Court restrict abortions by imposing parental or spousal notification, mandatory "counseling," or waiting periods. The results of the politics of compromise applied to the moral issue of abortion are fascinating: abortion is rendered feasible for the middle and upper classes but not for many of the poor and young. It is easy to see why neither the pro-choice nor the pro-life are satisfied with this policy. Here, the evolution of compromise through the processes of pluralistic politics generates an outcome that contains a palpable double standard. Compromise it is. Fair it is not. If we are to be increasingly concerned about morality and not simply divvying up material benefits, we need to look beyond the pluralist faith in the power of compromise and toward some more viable concept of majority rule.

At the heart of the inadequacies of American pluralism lies the question that famed pluralist Robert Dahl poses in the title of his most famous work: who governs? It seems increasingly evident that the best answer to this question is that, in America, no one governs.

The implications of this simple fact are rather astounding. Ours is not a particularly representational government. That our government heeds the will of no one at the expense of others is *not* equivalent to representing the people. Indeed, no one is represented by American government except in the very limited sense of having a voice heard but not acted upon (and to the extent that there is a will to avoid tyranny). Beyond that, however, we receive little representation. Pluralists are wrong to suggest that it is democratic when our government cannot readily proceed with policy in the absence of ultra-majoritarian support (that is, without support from far more than a simple majority in order to overcome the intense checks and balances of American politics). Indeed, it helps assure that America has one of the least representative governments among non-dictatorships.

There is nothing fundamentally new about this type of critique (an anti-pluralist critique) of American government. This theoretical perspective is sometimes labeled hyperpluralist theory instead of anti-pluralist theory, usually by those who do not subscribe to, or perhaps fully understand, the theory. The trouble with America isn't quite that we simply have *too much* pluralism. Either a government is pluralist or it is not. If it is pluralist, like ours, there will be problems. Theodore Lowi is perhaps the Political Scientist best known for arguing pluralist American government yields gridlock. In *The End of Liberalism*,[10] he claims that there is a plethora of special

What is the Alternative to Pluralism? Majoritarianism

The alternative to dispersing power (pluralism) is concentrating it and, unfortunately, the most obvious concentrations of power occur in dictatorships of all sorts. However, it is fully possible to concentrate power democratically by placing it in the hands of the majority. Most European parliamentary democracies do precisely that. Absent are the separations of power and checks and balances between them. Instead, whatever political party or parties can amass a majority of seats in parliament are firmly in charge as long as they can agree on how to govern or until they lose an election. The executive leaders do not constitute a separate branch of government. They are simultaneously the leaders of parliament, generally the most influential members of that institution. They fill positions such as Prime Minister and the key ministerial positions that head up the various executive departments precisely because they are the key members of parliament. In short, there is no separation between legislative and executive. The executive leaders are the leaders of parliament.

Truly non-pluralist representative government also features unicameralism (a unified or one-house legislature) and the absence of judicial review. There is no need to divide the legislature against itself if you believe that the majority is able and entitled to govern. Often, non-pluralist democracies have a second legislative chamber but its powers are typically merely advisory or consultative. Judicial review is also absent because the best protection of the rights of the people is assured by their democratic right to majority rule (unhindered by a supreme court that can strike down their will). Pluralist government is desired only by those who fear the people and their majority will. To be sure, the rights of minorities (both political and racial and ethnic) are no small matters but pluralism only offers the protections afforded by imposing weak and gridlock-bound government. Whenever minorities need prompt, effective government to secure their needs, pluralism is bound to prove more of a hindrance than a help.

Of course, pure and absolute majoritarianism may be something to fear or, at least, an object of concern. However, no political system is *purely* anything. Our pathological pluralist system does not disperse power all the time in every way imaginable. Similarly, majoritarian systems do not concentrate power in the hands of the majority all the time and in every way imaginable. European polities, for example, have various minor pluralist wrinkles and times when they require supra-majorities; the European Union has them in even greater abundance. However, here we are considering the general character of polities and the point not to be missed is that those polities that *generally* confer power to the majority are typically preferable to those that *generally* disperse power broadly and pit it against itself—thus pitting people against one another. Majoritarian politics is better able to generate public solutions to public problems and the responsiveness of government to public will encourages populations to be more thoughtful and careful about what they demand of their governments. Those who get what they want from government may have to be more careful about what they request.

interest groups that possess veto power to prevent changes they don't like, but that do not possess the positive power to generate constructive changes (however that might be defined). Because some of the reforms that Lowi recommends at the conclusion of his classic text seem to resurrect new instantiations of pluralism, perhaps the most consistently anti-pluralist classic text is Robert Paul Wolff's *The Poverty of Liberalism*.[11] By the way, neither Lowi nor Wolff are using the term liberalism in its everyday sense. They are referring to liberalism in the broader sense, as the political ideology that endorses pluralism (cultural and/or institutional), constitutionalism, and capitalism in its vision of representative government.

Wolff convincingly argues that government in America is fundamentally analogous to a traffic jam. The end result of so many groups trying to pull policy in different directions within a government structure that gives them every opportunity to thwart one another and requires relative consensus to overcome opposition, is that little is accomplished. Few ever decide that they want governmental gridlock any more than motorists take to the road to be part of a traffic jam. But the end result is that with so many people trying to go in so many directions at the same time, no one gets very far. Perhaps Wolff has just given us a more robust understanding of what other critics of pluralism called "mush." Nonetheless, the implication is clear. Americans are ruled by default. Our political system features considerable activity and effort, but little achievement. The problems that plague us most, our embarrassing record in health, education, safety, and economic opportunity, among others, are not the conscious failings of anyone. Instead, they are the inadvertent consequence of a political system that places too much of a premium on avoiding dictatorship and not enough on solving common problems. And, in the end, our unalleviated problems themselves become our tyrants.

Interestingly, the most popular critique of American government stems from elite theory, not anti-pluralist theory. Elite theory is rooted in the classic text of C. Wright Mills, *The Power Elite*.[12] Elite theory asserts that, in America, power is in fact concentrated in the hands of a wealthy elite who control most of what does and doesn't happen in our politics. The recommended remedy is reform that would break up their unfair control, by dispersing power (and wealth) so that we can have genuine pluralism for the first time. To be sure, there is tremendous evidence of classism and grotesque economic inequalities in America but it seems to me that elite theory is basically wrong in both of its most central propositions. First, the wealthy, however privileged, do not appear to have (or even need) political control. Wealth and privilege embedded in the status quo are protected to the extent that the status quo is assured. Second, we already have genuine pluralism. It is the reason we are mired in impotence. The empowerment of the non-rich would seem to require majoritarianism, not pluralism (a fact that did not elude Madison).

Even so, it is reasonable to ask if governmental impotence serves the interests of some better than others. It does. For example, weak government may have pleasant consequences, at least in the short run, if you are very rich and especially concerned that government not have the power or coordination to take away many of your advantages. In short, pluralism ensures the rich that they won't be saddled with ambitious redistributive policies, progressive taxation or, as in Madison's day, policies that advantage debtors over creditors. As a rich person, you may not control government but you do not need to. You will nonetheless be basically free from its control.

When government is weak and lacks the power to generate public solutions to public problems, individuals of means may choose to try to pursue *private* solutions to public problems. For example, if lakes and oceans are too polluted and government can't respond, you can always put in a swimming pool or vacation to a remote, non-polluted location. If crime is a problem and government can't respond, you can always buy a security system. If public schools are run down and inadequate and government can't respond, you can always go to a fancy private school. And so on. Two points need to be remembered. First, these private "solutions" are available only to the relatively rich. Those who need help to survive or who need redistributive policies to have a chance at a decent life, have as much reason to be horrified by the absence of stronger government as the rich have reason to rejoice in it. And, second, private initiatives are no real substitute for effective public responses to what is inherently a public problem. Because they are a means of evading problems rather than confronting them, they leave intact the dirt, the violence, and the decay that have a way of expanding and developing into new, farther reaching problems with often unforeseen consequences. In sum, one of the most basic roots of the trouble with America is our need for effective government and the incapacity of our current pluralist political structures to provide us with it.

NOTES

1. James Madison, "Federalist Paper Number 10," in Alexander Hamilton, James Madison, and John Jay, *The Federalist Papers*, ed. Clinton Rossiter (New York: Mentor, 1999), 49.

2. David F. Schuman with Bob Waterman, *A Preface to Politics*, 4th ed. (Lexington, MA: DC Heath & Co., 1986), 16.

3. Robert Paul Wolff, *The Poverty of Liberalism* (Boston: Beacon Press, 1968), 118.

4. Some Political Scientists may speak of "pluralism" merely as the manner in which all political systems come to terms with, and involve, diverse and conflicting

political communities. However, in this book, I use the term in its more conventional and theoretical sense: as a descriptor of the general character of a polity that disperses power via political structures and/or cultural diversity and that pits power against power, usually with the hope of avoiding tyranny presumed to be associated with powerful government.

5. James Madison, "Federalist Paper Number 51," in *The Federalist Papers*, 290.

6. Unlike a controversial predecessor, Bernard de Mandeville, Adam Smith did not argue that all public benefits arise from private vices. However, Smith did assert that the pursuit of private luxury could be beneficial to society generally. He did not believe that much good came from those who traded with the intent of serving the public good but instead argued that the rich, in their pursuit of pure selfishness, were forced to share some of their riches with the poor. For details, see James Buchan's very readable *The Authentic Adam Smith: His Life and Ideas* (New York: Norton, 2006), 19–20, 94, and 62–63.

7. Adam Smith considered himself at least as much of a moral philosopher as an economist. When it came to the latter, he was not a simple free trade advocate but instead approved of some restraints on trade, monopolies, subsidies, interest rate limits, etc. He never once used the words *laissez faire* in *The Wealth of Nations* and he never used the phrase "invisible hand" in any discussion unambiguously about market capitalism. He did, however, argue that trade initiated from selfish desires generally contributed more to the public good than trade attempted with the intent of serving the public good. See Buchan, *The Authentic Adam Smith*, 2–3 and 63.

8. Robert Dahl, *Who Governs?* 9th ed. (New Haven: Yale University Press, 1979).

9. Paul H. Appleby used the term "mesh" in his book, *Policy and Administration* (Tuscaloosa, AL: University of Alabama Press, 1949), 47. However, he expresses his pluralist view more articulately in *Morality and Administration in Democratic Government* (Baton Rouge, LA: LSU Press, 1952), 173: "Nothing is so representative of the public as the product of the totality of our political processes."

10. Theodore J. Lowi, *The End of Liberalism*, 2nd ed. (New York: Norton, 1979).

11. Wolff, *The Poverty of Liberalism*.

12. C. Wright Mills, *The Power Elite*, (New York: Oxford University Press, 2000/1956).

2

Constitutionalism and the Limitation of Virtue

Restraint. That is the essence of it. Students of American government from every corner of the country sit down to learn that the principal virtue of American government, the principal source of our core freedoms—freedom of speech, freedom of press, freedom of assembly and of the right to petition, freedom of religion and more—is the restraint of government, that is, constitutionalism, the limitation of government authority and power. It sounds wonderful. But wait a second. Restraint? American government is restrained? The government that seems addicted to war, that is constantly acting unilaterally, warring, invading countries, CIA coup plotting and coup staging; the government that through such actions has killed more people than any other currently in existence;[1] the government that whisks people off streets, typically on the basis of false and incomplete information, and assassinates them or sends them off to be tortured and killed or released years later without so much as an apology; the government that has toppled more democracies, and many non-democracies as well, than any other government on the planet; the government that befriends and eggs on regimes that are among the most (not the least) likely to murder, torture, and disempower the bulk of their own populations—*that* government is *restrained*?

Well, in *some* ways American government *is* restrained. As we saw in the previous chapter, American government is restrained in its ability to generate public solutions to our public problems, to implement policies, to make America and the world better places. But even when it comes to those wonderful assurances about our individual freedoms—speech, press, assembly, etc.—so often the focus of the typical lecture on constitutionalism, the sad bottom line is that these limitations on our government's abusiveness directed against our own population are *not* nearly as solid or real or secure

23

as the vast majority of Americans have been led to believe. Post–9/11, the PATRIOT Act and similar "emergency" measures have been widely acknowledged as restraining individual freedom but such freedom was tenuous in many significant ways long before.

What *is*, and always has been, principally limited by American constitutionalism is not vice, not the abuse of ordinary Americans, but virtue, the ability to meet their needs. Paradoxically, ours is a government incapable of genuinely democratic processes in which majorities regularly and reliably direct government solutions to our common problems, yet ours is also a government nonetheless perfectly capable of warring against and destroying such practices when they occur elsewhere. Ours is a government where the meaning of core individual freedoms is subject to such vague and easily twisted or amended constitutional interpretations that these "freedoms" serve to protect us best when we need no protection at all and protect us far less when we desperately need it. This then is the core problem of American constitutionalism: the only thing it limits with reliability and effectiveness is governmental virtue.

Apologists for constitutionalism are apt to point first and foremost to the first amendment as an outstanding example of the importance and effectiveness of limiting governmental power. This, it is said, is America's crowning glory: a guarantee of core civil liberties, the very life blood of a democracy. And of the core freedoms "assured" there, freedom of religion, speech, press, assembly, and petition, what seems most central to contemporary Americans is freedom of speech. This may be the cornerstone freedom of American "democracy," the civil liberty most basic and most treasured insofar as it is hard to imagine any meaningful governmental representation of public will without it. It is interesting to note that the constitution's framers listed freedom of religion first and freedom of speech only second, and that they opposed the idea of a Bill of Rights but were pressured into it by opponents of the constitution who would not support it without such amendments. Perhaps early Americans, especially those fearful of the new government's potential power, were more concerned about religious expression than political expression per se and, in a more secular era, perhaps the reverse is true now, but it is certainly fair to say that all of these "liberties" are important and entwined. But let's take a look at what modern Americans probably consider most central of all, freedom of speech, and examine the limitations on the limitations of government, the restraints on governmental restraint.

Start with a good look at the constitutional language that "provides" our speech rights: "Congress shall make no law . . . abridging the freedom of speech . . ." Read it again: "*Congress* shall make no law . . ." Is the American "liberty" of speech *solely* a protection against the potential intrusion of Congress? Ultimately, the answer to that is "no," but because of the complexities of the evolution of constitutional law and interpretation and the vagaries of executive branch and state government assaults on speech rights, the answer is far more complex than generally acknowledged in introductory texts on American government. Many a president has created an enemies list based on who spoke out publicly against his policies. Such actions are typically secret and go undetected; however, Woodrow Wilson and Richard Nixon are well-known examples. The Wilson administration had the Justice Department sponsor a nationwide vigilante organization, the American Protective League, which read the mail of "disloyals," infiltrated private meetings and kept "verbatim" notes on their public speeches—all of which was used to try to find a basis for bringing federal charges based on the Espionage Act of 1917 & 1918, which imposed prison sentences of up to 20 years on over 900 individuals convicted of speech acts "disruptive" to military enlistment or expressing anything "disloyal, scornful, or contemptuous" of the U.S. government.[2] Richard Nixon's enemies list was also drawn on the basis of who dared to speak against his administration. Nixon used the list to direct the Internal Revenue Service to engage in tax audits of individuals on the list and to order the Federal Bureau of Investigation to direct wiretapping and other electronic surveillance against them. The courts never ruled on the former but in United States v. U.S. District Court (1972), the Supreme Court ruled that, without probable cause or judicial approval, such surveillance violated the Fourth Amendment's prohibition against unreasonable searches. The case was not decided on first amendment speech issues. In the post–9/11, post–PATRIOT Act environment in which George W. Bush declared war against all those who were and are "not with us" in the struggle against "terrorism," it is unlikely that criticism of the president will always be considered insufficient grounds for government surveillance. While the aforementioned cases involve a president initiating a serious assault on free speech, it is clear that these abuses are only made effective in tandem with laws passed by Congress: for Wilson it was the Espionage Act and for Nixon it was the statutes enabling IRS audits and FBI investigations. As such, they can come under the rubric of the first amendment's semi-protections of free speech if the courts do what they have *not* consistently done: interpret the first amendment in a civil libertarian manner.

The states are another potential source of abridgement of speech rights. The constitution was created as a limitation upon *national* governmental power. In early American history, the courts affirmed time and time again, most famously in Barron v. Baltimore (1833), that the constitution's Bill of Rights/civil liberties restraints on government apply only to the national government. The 1848 Fourteenth Amendment opened the possibility of applying these restraints to the states with its pivotal passage: "No state shall make or enforce any law which shall abridge the privileges or immunities of citizens of the United States." Through a slow and arduous process of case-by-case "selective incorporation," starting in 1897 and ending in 1969, most of the amendments in the Bill of Rights have been imposed on the states, with a majority of the decisions coming between 1962 and 1969, during the aberrational liberal Warren Court years. A couple of things are especially noteworthy in this history. First, for the bulk of American history, the states could be and were quite a menace to civil liberty; even the limited scope of freedom we now enjoy is a relatively recent phenomenon. Second, Gitlow v. New York (1925), which was the first case to feature a majority opinion that asserted that the constitution's freedom of speech provision applies to the states, was, nonetheless, on balance, most significant as a profound *assault* on American speech rights. Benjamin Gitlow was a socialist who in word and in print called for a vague proletarian struggle against capitalism while specifically disavowing any immediate revolution. The Gitlow Supreme Court ruling *upheld* New York State's criminal anarchy law and Gitlow's conviction under it, even though New York did not even attempt to show that Gitlow's speech posed any danger. The court "reasoned" that Gitlow's remarks might contribute to igniting a revolutionary act at some point in the future. As we continue to see how weak American speech rights have been and remain, it is of relatively little comfort that *these* minimum protections can now be imposed upon the states.

Still, probably the biggest gap in American free speech is not that it is rooted in language that doesn't specify the executive branch or the states. Those gaps have been, by and large, somewhat filled by modern Supreme Court rulings. Rather, the biggest problem is that American political theory and practice *un*reasonably assumes that the only, or primary, source of assault on liberty is government. Put another way, Americans have a one-sided and foolish concept of freedom as something that can be guaranteed by limiting *government*. But there is another, far more dangerous source of the manipulation of individuals and the abridgement of their liberty: the *private* sector, ranging from other individuals and common opinion and prejudice to, most nefarious of all, employers. This is a critical point: focusing all efforts on the "restraint" of government leaves intact all non-governmental sources of infringement upon the rights of individuals. One does not need to be extremely well versed in American history to realize that the most dangerous and, thus, most punished utterances sounded less like *We should vote for Gus Hall* (Hall was the quadrennial Communist Party presidential candidate from 1972 to 1984) and much more like: *Why do we do all the work and the owner gets all the money? Why are Pinkertons brought in to beat the crap out of us every time we ask for a living wage?* and, most of all, *We should try to form a union.* In the current era, both Pinkerton "armies" of private guards-for-hire and unionization efforts are a lot less common. So, too, are decent jobs. What *is* ubiquitous is the fear of pink slips. Americans have been told over and over again, from grade school on, that we have free speech here in this country and yet they generally remain keenly aware that saying whatever you want in the workplace is a formula for disaster. What is painfully absent from American policy is something like Sweden's Employment Security Act of 1974 which significantly restricts employers' ability to dismiss workers. This is the reason why Swedes have a lot more free speech rights than Americans.

Political Scientist David Schuman has aptly described the problem this way: Americans have a respectable amount of "freedom from" but distressing little "freedom to."³ In other words, Americans suffer from a one-dimensional concept of freedom in which it is assumed, falsely, that the restraint of government interference, to the diluted extent we have that, assures individual autonomy. A staunch critic of pluralism, Schuman notes that freedom from tyranny does *not* assure freedom to live in meaningful community, to prosper, and to be happy. Since the distinction between "freedom from" and "freedom to" is largely semantic—in other words, freedom from censorship and freedom to speak are essentially the same— perhaps it is more useful to make the distinction in a slightly different way, namely, ordinary Americans have some measure of freedom from government but remarkably little freedom *via* government. Sweden, by contrast, seems to have relatively little trouble realizing that the only way to assure free speech involves both avoiding government censorship of, or sanction against, free speech *and* using relatively more powerful government to restrain private and business imposed censorship and sanction. A related worry concerns the current lack of public space altogether. In previous generations, it was relatively easy to get a soap box, bring it to a public downtown corner, stand on it, and address passersby. Such public rhetoric is a thing of the past. Today, Americans gather and pass primarily in private space (e.g., shopping malls) where public speech is neither protected nor allowed.⁴

A prime indicator that something is seriously wrong with the *scope* of free speech in America is the fact that Americans hold remarkably similar and conformist opinions. For all the news show chatter about the great divide between red states and blue states, between conservatives and liberals, the overwhelming majority of Americans share an unquestioning faith in that which is so questionable: the core structure of American politics as a limited (pluralist and constitutionalist) representative government within a capitalist economy. The only thing that differentiates one from another are issues of fine tuning (e.g., Should constitutionalist decisions be made with judicial activism or restraint? How much public financing should we have in our plurality elections? or How much regulation should be integrated into capitalism? etc.). In short, America is a uni-ideological society; virtually all Americans ascribe to liberalism *in the broad*, not narrow, sense—endorsing pluralism, constitutionalism, and capitalism as defining features of their flawed conception of representational politics. In the absence of a vibrant, reflective, and informed political life such conformity of opinion is more an indication of a problem than a source of comfort.

As early as 1835, Alexis de Tocqueville, with an outsider's eyes, famously noted in *Democracy in America*, that one of the most obvious characteristics of the American republic was this unhealthy leveling of opinion. He called it a tyranny of the majority but it was really much more than that; it was a conformity that extended well beyond the bounds of a simple majority. In the America of today, this leveling of, or uniformity of, opinion may be even more problematic and may be compounded by the unique characteristics of a truly mass media. It is nearly Orwellian that the overwhelming majority of Americans so often go from having never heard of a Mohmmar Qaddafi or Osama bin Laden to, within a matter of hours, thinking that they do know who he is and that he approximates the devil incarnate. At the time I write this, bin Laden is the ultimate *persona non grata* for Americans. Who, in such a climate, would *not* be fearful of saying *I kind of like Osama*? We all know that it would be extremely dangerous to utter that idea. In previous decades it was Menachum Begin, Yassir Arafat, or Qaddafi who were demonized; later, of course, they were championed as important and helpful allies. In other words and crudely put, Americans toe "the party line" without the party. This is not what one would intuitively anticipate from a society that genuinely treasures freedom of expression.

Perhaps all that is new is the speed at which mass media generates mass opinion. However, I think there is something unique about the degree to which television in particular has saturated American life. The typical American now watches an average of four hours of television per day—more on the weekend and less on weekdays, but on average, four hours daily. It may be more than hyperbole to wonder if Americans themselves aren't programmed. If the program contents are not of concern, commercials themselves, explicitly designed to alter viewer behavior, are an enormous part of the problem. With the typical American lifespan extending beyond eighty, it is accurate to estimate that the ordinary American is watching about fourteen *solid* years (no sleep time included in the calculations) of television. With commercials now comprising one-third of all air time, the typical American is spending well over four and a half *solid* years of time just watching commercials. These are staggering numbers and they reflect a tremendous amount of time spent being essentially passive and subject to the *programming* of others. Perhaps Americans' largest problem is not limited freedom of speech per se, but a lack of speech altogether.

Even so, the typical text on American politics or constitutional law essentially ignores these concerns about the curtailment of free speech by leveled opinion, mass media, employers, etc. From the mainstream perspective, the first amendment government-oriented protection of speech is, well, good enough—good enough to secure a society that may not be ideally free but is rather sufficiently free. Unfortunately, a careful examination of free speech case law and legal precedents reveals that American speech rights are most fragile when they are most needed and quite far from good enough to secure a truly open and democratic society. Even if we proceed with the false and unwarranted assumption that the only real threats to free speech come from government, our courts, over the years, have *not* done a very good job of consistently restraining government abridgements of speech.

In Schenck v. United States (1919), the Supreme Court upheld the conviction of Charles Schenck, equating Schenck's speech with "yelling fire in a crowded theater," something that presented a *clear and present danger* to others. In fact, what Schenck had done was distribute leaflets that opposed the draft, arguing that it constituted involuntary servitude and, as such, violated the Thirteenth Amendment. The court ruled that the government may be especially restrictive of speech during times of war—a precedent of some grave concern in the current "war on terror" which seems to impose a permanent state of war. One week after issuing the Schenck verdict, the court upheld the conviction of Socialist Party leader Eugene Debs for criticizing the government's incarceration of several people who made anti-war speeches. Especially deplorable was the ten year sentence imposed on Rose Pastor Stokes for declaring "I am for the people and the government is for the profiteers."[5] Debs had not advocated draft resistance but his conviction was upheld anyway on the grounds that together with his party's public opposition to World War I, his words had a "bad tendency," asserting, rather implausibly, that they tended to make military recruitment more difficult. This "bad tendency test," which seemed to allow almost anyone to be imprisoned for saying anything the least bit critical of government or elites, was formalized with Abrams v. United States (also 1919), which upheld the conviction of Jacob Abrams for distributing leaflets urging workers to resist American military intervention in Russia. The court suggested Abrams's words *might* lead to a general strike, which *might* limit ordnance production.

We have already seen that, in Gitlow v. New York (1925), the Supreme Court ruled that individuals can be incarcerated for any speech that could conceivably contribute to any revolutionary act at any future point (with a very strange and broad notion of "could conceivably contribute"). Gitlow, for example, was incarcerated for calling for an eventual long-term struggle against capitalism. In Whitney v. California (1927), the Supreme Court upheld the conviction of Charlotte Anita Whitney under California's Criminal Syndicalism Act. Whitney had advocated electoral politics (voting) as a means of class struggle. On the basis of her membership in the Communist Labor Party, Whitney was convicted for belonging to an organization that presented a "bad tendency," that *might* promote unlawful acts at some point in time.

In Dennis v. United States (1951), the Supreme Court developed a new standard, the clear and *probable* danger test, one which would be used to restrict only speech that they deemed *likely* to be dangerous, not just possibly dangerous. Here, however, the Supreme Court upheld the constitutionality of the Smith Act, which made it a crime to merely advocate the overthrow of *any* government in the United States. Moreover, Eugene Dennis never did that. Like virtually all members of the Communist Party, he argued that revolution was many decades in the future. That point, however, was lost on the Supreme Court. They took membership in any "communist party" to be prima facie evidence of advocacy of the overthrow of the U.S. government.[6] By the late '50s and early '60s, convictions under the Dennis precedent were restricted to *active* members of such parties but the Court did not move away from its bizarre and self-imposed notion of what constitutes advocacy of government overthrow. Also in the wake of the Dennis ruling, the Supreme Court invented an ad hoc balancing standard, not so much a clear interpretive doctrine but rather a general judicial decision-making guideline, one wherein the court would try to weigh the competing "private" interest in having free speech against the "public" interest in restricting it. Like the clear and probable danger test, this was based on strange and prejudicial notions of what was dangerous and allowed for a wide array of profound limitations on speech rights.

It wasn't until 1969 that the Supreme Court explicitly overturned Whitney v. California and thus, for the first time, refused to sanction the incarceration of someone for belonging to a political party presumed by nonmembers to be promoting unlawful conduct. In Brandenburg v. Ohio (1969), the court reversed the conviction of local Ku Klux Klan leader Clarence Brandenburg, coming full circle back to the clear and *present* danger, this time asserting that a danger to the public welfare is only really present if speech is inciting of *imminent* (immediately at hand) lawless action. However, if this history is to be understood properly, it must be clear that relative restrictions on speech do not ebb and flow in a generally uniform direction from greater to lesser restrictions. Rather, they reflect the prejudices and paranoias of their day, namely, at the time, how fearful and hateful is government (and its judges) of anarchism, socialism, pacifism, communism, and, of course now, Islamism. The legacy of America's quite limited speech rights is not only that the aforementioned convictions were allowed to stand in their time (when the key social prejudices were antileftist) but also rather that the principles upon which they rest *still stand*. Whatever is judged by the prejudices of our time to invoke a "bad tendency" or to present a clear and *possible* or *probable* or *present* or *imminent* danger (and the standard from one to the other shifts quickly with the scope of our societal fear and prejudice at the time, very much reflected in the courts and its verdicts) is *not* allowed and those who utter such things are indeed prone to arrest, conviction, and incarceration. While the constitutionality of the craze of post–9/11 measures may not be fully determined for many years, what is clear is that a court system that once confused simple membership in any socialist party with conspiracy to violently overthrow the government is now free to confuse madrases (which simply means school) with terrorist training camps and jihad (which simply means struggle to improve oneself) with violent terrorist organizations—making those who advocate either very much subject to a new era's prejudices and punishments and the mitigated speech rights that accompany them.

So, it is almost certainly the case that American speech rights are not nearly as potent or as safe as the typical American supposes. In fact, these judicial standards, ranging from the clear and present danger test to the bad tendency test, are particularly worrisome insofar as they seem to suggest that speech is protected best when it matters least and protected least when it matters most. Think of it this way: if a political speech occurs in a climate of crisis and the speech is persuasive and both commands attention and evokes a will to make significant change in the current order of things, then it will be easiest to argue that the speech is dangerous—dangerous at least to those invested in the status quo and fearful of significant change. If a political speech occurs in a climate when there is no mood for change or simply a complacency of stifling disaffection from activism or if a speech is just particularly inefficacious or inoffensive to anyone, then it will be most likely to be deemed innocuous rather than dangerous. Have American free speech rights degenerated to this sad state of affairs? You can say whatever you want so long as no one is listening or apt to agree or to be stirred to action?

It is perhaps most intriguing that American courts have been as restrictive of speech as they have, given an American political system that stymies movement and change via pluralism (to guarantee constant oppositions to almost any initiative) and constitutionalism (which better limits government's ability to accomplish good than its ability to restrict those who champion it). In short, Americans can be expected to be a remarkably apathetic and disengaged lot given these systemic bulwarks against change, given the numbing effects of frustration after frustration for those who expect that American government will respond as well to public initiative as its more vibrant representative (*non*-pluralist) counterparts in Europe and elsewhere. Public orators have an awful lot to overcome and one of the things that makes so laughable the court's various assertions about the horrific dangers of lecturers and orators (and non-mainstream ones at that) is how far-fetched it seems that these puddles of opposition could have overturned governments and war-mongering in America. And yet, these champions of change, when they were not incarcerated, were subject to other sundry forms of assault and harassment by government—all without a decisive protective barrier in the constitution. For example, populist songster Joe Hill was falsely convicted on trumped-up murder charges and executed by the state of Utah. Anarchists Alexander Berkman and Emma Goldman were deported to communist Russia—even though neither had ever come from there. Filmmaker and movie star Charlie Chaplin was deported ostensibly on "morals" charges for marrying a much younger woman but really because of the socialist themes in his very popular movies. Singing sensation Paul Robeson was blacklisted, largely at the government's initiative, for championing civil rights and the rights of the poor. Singer, songwriter, and former Beatles star John Lennon faced ongoing wiretaps and harassments and deportation proceedings ostensibly for a minor drug violation years and years earlier but really because of his left-leaning politics. In short, the FBI was primarily attempting to stop dissent, even within a political climate where such dissent was nascent and inconsequential. Sadly, the constitution does not often seem to arise, in such cases, as a prompt and efficacious protection of dissent.

There are many liberties in American politics, which like our speech rights, are not fully protected by restraining government alone, especially when the restraint of government in these areas is fairly meager and lackluster. Such partially protected liberties may include other first amendment freedoms (freedom of press, assembly, petition, and freedom of and from religion) and the core protections of the rights of the accused found elsewhere within the Bill of Rights (e.g., the protection against unreasonable search and seizure, the right to competent counsel, etc.). Just a few examples follow: American press rights are compromised by increasingly monopolized ownership patterns. The increased ownership of American media outlets by very conservative owners, most notoriously Rupert Murdoch, is offset slightly by the mildly liberal political preferences of most reporters, at least those reporters who work for more mainstream news companies that don't, like Murdoch's, impose strict editorial guidelines to ensure the partisanship of news stories. However, the problems with American media extend far beyond the increasingly large segment of news outlets owned by conservative activists (e.g., Clear Channel Radio and Fox News). American media, unlike most of its European counterparts, does *not* offer a wide diversity of ideological perspectives. In part, this is due to the leveling of opinion de Tocqueville and others observed and worried about: the disinclination or inability of overwhelming majorities of Americans to question the basic ideological paradigm of the country or any of the core political structures (such as pluralism, constitutionalism, and capitalism). In part, too, American media has been more readily controlled or influenced by government in the post-Vietnam era as presidents and other national politicians have worked successfully to limit media access (particularly access to war zones), have made clear that access to other stories is contingent upon favorable or sympathetic coverage of U.S. warfare, and have cautioned news companies about possible public anger about any news stories that might appear to undermine war efforts. The most famous example of this problem may be the case of video journalist Jon Alpert who, in the first Gulf War, shot footage of hundreds upon hundreds of Iraqi civilians killed in American bombings, undermining mainstream American news stories that strongly and falsely suggested that there were fewer civilian fatalities than military ones in that war.[7] Producer after producer who agreed to air Alpert's work was fired from the various networks. Alpert's story appeared throughout Europe and the world, winning him many awards and honors, but it never aired in the United States. A media free from formal censorship but nonetheless generally uni-ideological and often politically and socially co-opted is hardly a press capable of adequately informing a citizenry.

American assembly and petition rights are increasingly fractured by the biases of both a society and a government quick to suspect guilt by association, especially when they have prejudices against various kinds of associations. Freedom *from* religion, the protection of the rights of atheists and agnostics, has never been supported here as well as freedom *of* religion has been, but even the latter is incomplete when a group is marginalized, feared, and/or hated as Muslims seem to be now. The standards for what is and is not reasonable in search and seizure depends at least as much on who is being searched and what is being seized than on the nature and qualities of the process, both reflecting and rendering serious classist and racist biases. These search and seizure practices reflect all the same problems that undermine free speech rights: suspicion of illegal activity is often based more on a prejudice about a particular group, prejudice reflected in both courts and court ordered warrants, than upon actual observations of genuinely illegal or truly suspicious activities. At times, courts don't even attempt to hide the double standards in play here. For example, in Illinois v. Wardlow (2000), the Supreme Court ruled that running from police officers is by itself sufficient grounds for an immediate legal search and seizure but only if it occurs in a "high crime area." (Sam Wardlow ran when police cruisers pulled up rapidly in front of him while investigating a matter totally unrelated to him. It was Wardlow's fleeing alone that prompted the police pursuit and search of him.) The court never examined what was and wasn't a "high crime area." They simply assumed that if it's a neighborhood that was largely poor and non-Caucasian, it was a "high crime area" and they would never consider applying this ruling to, let's say, the Financial District (Wall Street) in New York City where the rate of "white collar" crimes is so high that it is undoubtedly one of the highest crime areas in the country.[8] Legal outcomes often are more a reflection of the caliber of attorneys than of the merits of the case at hand and the many who depend upon public or even merely affordable defenders, are far from assured of *competent* counsel.

No, inadequate speech rights are not the end all and be all of the problems with American constitutionalism. They are, however, particularly emblematic. What better example than free speech, arguably the cornerstone of American freedoms, the one upon which participatory democracy itself seems most dependent, as an American ideal which everywhere receives lip service but is a right that remains at core only partially protected because the defenses of it are all erected against possible government, not other, intrusions, and because those defenses are fairly shoddily and inconsistently erected even against governmental abuses?

If the U.S. Constitution does a lackluster job protecting speech and dissent, are there any areas where its restrictions on government are far more potent? Certainly yes, but sadly those areas tend to be the protection of large-scale private property and its holders. Ultimately, perhaps it should not be surprising that, compared to its tenuous civil liberty protections, the U.S. Constitution has always imposed more formidable and more consistent restraints upon government regulation of business, making protection of the public interest, defense of the ordinary person, and promotion of virtue generally *more* difficult.[9] The Bill of Rights, after all, was a bit of an afterthought, a political *concession* somewhat reluctantly granted by the Federalists to those anti-Federalists who, with just a bit more reassurance, might eventually agree to sign on for the adoption of the constitution as it began to appear more and more likely to be enacted.

From the beginning of the nineteenth century forward, the contracts clause of Article I, Section 10 of the constitution became the basis of the Supreme Court's invalidation of most significant state regulations of business. The contracts clause forbids states from "impairing the obligation of contracts" and it became the "justification" for a first great era of conservative judicial activism that expanded the scope of laissez-faire capitalism. By the 1880s and well into the twentieth century, the due process clause of the Fourteenth Amendment became the key basis of the Court's assault on state regulation of business. The due process clause prohibits states from depriving a person of life, liberty, or *property* without due process of the law. The same section, section one, of the Fourteenth Amendment extended all privileges and immunities of citizens of the United States to all the states. Critically important to understanding the full significance of this change is the realization that the courts defined corporations as *individuals*, as possessing all the rights of citizens. In short, the Fourteenth Amendment has become a formidable bulwark against state regulation of business, though, on the surface, it was a post–Civil War protection of the rights of freed slaves. How poorly freed slaves fared and were treated strongly suggests that the Fourteenth Amendment's larger significance lies elsewhere—specifically, in the protection of big business. It is perhaps particularly ironic that the due process clause has become the tool of preference for a new and current generation of conservative judicial activists who have used the due process clause to shut down an electoral recount (in Bush v. Gore, 2000) and, irony of ironies, to strike down racial desegregation (in Parents Involved in Community Schools v. Seattle School District No. 1 and Meredith v. Jefferson County Kentucky Board of Education, 2007), arguing that singling out children for school reassignment largely on the basis of race does *not* provide them with equal treatment. This may be just the latest variant on an old argument that was used to obstruct civil rights proposals, namely, that protective legislation treats those to be protected differently from others and is therefore providing special rights or special privileges. It is a particularly bad argument but it has found much institutional support in olden days and, of course, again now.

Historically speaking, with the sole exception of the Warren Court years (1953–1969), the U.S. Supreme Court and the federal court system generally have been, as the judicial branch, the most conservative branch of American government. Perhaps this should not be surprising. Our legal system has built within it many conservative biases. One of them may be constitutionalism itself which contains within it a presumption that a government that governs least governs best and which forgets that to remove only public assaults on liberty is to leave intact all the myriad *private* assaults on liberty which could only be corralled by a government powerful enough to govern more, not less. In essence, this may be the heart of where the trouble with constitutionalism lies.

Still, there are many more bases of conservative bias in our court system. The lifetime tenures and insulation from public opinion and accountability play a role. More significant, however, may be the role of money within the legal process itself. Defense attorneys themselves are generally quick to point out that a defendant is typically better off being guilty but with enough money to afford excellent counsel than being innocent but dependent upon a public defender or weaker counsel. In civil suits, the question of quality of attorney is accompanied by concerns about the expense of both the process and outcome. Essentially, civil litigation in America has become a big game of chicken. The costs of engaging in a suit as plaintiff or defendant mount and mount as the process progresses and there are many opportunities for the more affluent party to delay and delay, driving up costs and putting pressure on the opposing party to settle or cave in. Intrinsically, this is a process that favors the rich over the poor. The very slowness of the process imposes costs and pressures more difficult to bear in direct relation to the degree of financial pressure a litigant feels. Added to these conservative or pro-monied inter-

What is the Alternative to Constitutionalism? Democracy

If you ask most Americans about the constitution they'll say, *It's wonderful! It's fabulous! It's the best thing since sliced bread!* If you ask them what's in it, they might have a general idea about one or two of its central aspects, but the main thrust of their answer will probably be, *I don't know.* This is itself a bit troubling and more than a little ironic. Still more interesting, however, is the American public's failure to realize that their love of constitution seems to directly contradict something even more central to their belief structure about what American government is and should be, namely, democratic. Think of it this way: without knowing much detailed content, Americans love a constitution that, in essence, restrains government. But, what they like best about the American political ideal is that it "is" democratic—a political system that is supposedly held accountable to, and must respond favorably to, what the people want and the ways they direct government to act. It is hard to imagine two American ideals more directly in contradiction of one another. If American government is and should be democratic, why would we want to restrain it? Isn't that just a restraint of ourselves and our own wants? Of course, apologists for pluralism love the contradiction; they champion a political system that is representative but not quite democratic, one that is somewhat responsive but not quite democratic, one that is somewhat responsive to public input but not too much so and not in ways that infringe too much upon "minority" rights (e.g., the rights of the propertied, minority religious groups, etc.). Perhaps many Americans like the idea of *other* Americans being restrained even better than they like the idea of being personally unrestrained and better than the idea of having a genuine democracy. Most likely, however, most Americans are largely unaware that a contradiction is present here at all.

Strictly speaking, the alternative to a constitutionalist polity is a nonconstitutionalist one where there are no special institutionalized restraints upon the government other than the restraints built into the everyday political process and environment itself: for example, and this varies widely with the nature of the polity, who holds power, how much power they have, what opposing powers and pressures they have to contend with, etc. In a representative political system, a non-constitutionalist system will entrust power to whatever party or parties hold(s) the reigns of government and it will be their desire to continue to govern that will force them to consider opposition parties, as well as ever-changing public input. Generally speaking, this is more effective and more responsive government than what is found in its constitutionalist counterparts. It is, in a word, something our founding fathers explicitly *rejected* in favor of their coveted tandem of pluralism and constitutionalism: democracy.

est biases are problems in attaining judicial standing. Essentially, in order to bring suit for damages imposed by a business, a prospective litigant must be able to demonstrate that large losses were imposed upon her or him personally. Class action suits are a theoretical possibility but new legal interpretations have made these suits harder to bring forward and more difficult to win. In short, the legal process itself favors those who do a little-to-moderate amount of harm to a great many people (i.e., corporations) over those who do a moderate-to-greater amount of harm to one or a few people (i.e. common criminals).

Of late, civil libertarians in America have been rightly concerned about the daunting effects of post–9/11 "anti-terrorist" measures like the PATRIOT Act and others. To be sure, there is much to be worried about here: the wide scale and apparently prejudicial arrests of hundreds of non-citizens; indefinite long-term incarceration without charges, without counsel, and even without notification of family; the use of torture against "enemy combatants" apparently rounded up haphazardly or even randomly (Guantanamo and Abu Ghraib are only the most infamous examples here);[10] wide scale indiscriminate surveillance of wireless telephone and internet communications; covert entries for the placement of keystroke loggers on computer keyboards; roving wiretaps authorized without probable cause; and the monitoring of the citizenry's library loan and book purchase reading selections, etc. Clearly, even if our courts, many years after the fact (as is typical) get around to striking down many of these practices,[11] this is *not* a country that has a particularly respectable record of civil liberty. Still, it would be a mistake to conclude that America has only gone awry post–9/11. The roots of America's woes are not in the inconsistent application of constitutionalism, but rather in constitutionalism itself. Constitutionalism in America has rendered a polity that lacks the power to protect us from corporate assaults upon our well-being, lacks the judicial principles upon which genuine freedom (such as free speech) rests, lacks the economic equality which, as we will see next, is an essential precursor to meaningful political equality and rights, and lacks the fortitude to apply to non-citizens even a pretense of the rudiments to the same basic rights we Americans at least profess to love.

NOTES

1. While some might consider Nazi Germany or Stalinist Russia the worst offenders in this regard, these regimes, thankfully, no longer exist. By contrast, the U.S. government endures and not only had a hand in the killings that were an integral part of World War II, but also in the killings of millions in Korea, Vietnam, and in the "lesser" invasions and/or bombings of Iraq, Afghanistan, Serbia, Panama, and so on, not to mention the government's role in the genocides of Native Americans and African slaves and the massive deaths associated with the Civil War.

2. For a detailed account of this, see Peter Irons, *A People's History of the Supreme Court* (New York: Penguin, 1999), 265–68.

3. David Schuman and Rex Wirth, *A Preface to Politics*, 6th ed. (Novato, CA: Chandler & Sharp, 2004), 185–210.

4. Some may consider the internet the new space for public speech. The problem here, however, is that such communication, like cell phone communication, is constantly subject to government surveillance by supercomputers searching for phrases indicative of radicalism, especially Islamism.

5. As cited in Irons, *A People's History*, 273.

6. For a detailed account of these cases, from Schenck to Dennis and beyond, again see Irons, *A People's History*.

7. Michael Hoy, "Jon Alpert: NBC's Odd Man Out," *Columbia Journalism Review* 30, no. 3 (September 1991): 44–47.

8. See Lenese C. Herbert, "Can't You See What I'm Saying? Making Expressive Conduct a Crime in High Crime Areas," *Georgetown Journal on Poverty Law & Policy* 9, no. 135 (2002): 138–45 and Lenese C. Herbert, "Bête Noire: How Race-Based Policing Threatens National Security," *Michigan Journal of Race and Law* 9 (2003): 149–213.

9. The classic two-volume scholarly work tracing American constitutional law's development as a legal system subordinating individual freedom to commercial, industrial, and corporate interests is Morton J. Horwitz's *The Transformation of American Law, 1780–1860* (Cambridge: Harvard University Press, 1977) and *The Transformation of American Law, 1870–1960* (New York: Oxford University Press, 1992). Page 253 of the first volume offers a concise statement of the thesis that this subordination intensified and became fully entrenched in the early 19th century.

10. The prisoners at Abu Ghraib prison in Iraq and at the Guantanamo naval base in the U.S.-occupied portion of Cuba were rounded up largely at random. American officials hoped that they were imprisoning, at Abu Ghraib, significant numbers of Iraqi resistance fighters and, at Guantanamo, significant numbers of Al Qaeda partisans. Photographs of Abu Ghraib prisoner abuse brought the scandal to public light and proved especially embarrassing because the torture involved sexual abuse (assumed to be particularly humiliating to Muslim victims). Prisoners in both locations are being held indefinitely without charges and being subjected to torture. For a detailed account of the random and arbitrary nature of the incarcerations at Guantanamo and Abu Ghraib, see Seymour M. Hersh, *Chain of Command: The Road from 9/11 to Abu Ghraib* (New York: HarperCollins, 2004).

11. The June 2008 Supreme Court ruling in Boumediene et. al. v. Bush et. al., which allows non-citizens to access the courts to contest the legality of their incarceration and abuse, is probably, at this writing, the most significant step in reeling in some of the post–9/11 infringements on civil liberty. However, if past history is a guide, such fluxes in the extent of civil liberty abuse are likely to ebb and flow, never affording adequate protection for ordinary Americans and non-citizens. The scope of civil liberty is generally minimal in the times of turmoil when logic would dictate it is needed most and most liberal in times of acquiescence when it is needed less.

3

Capitalism and the Ethos of Greed

Protect everything, detect everything, contain everything—obsessional society. Save time. Save energy. Save money. Save our souls—phobic society. Low tar. Low energy. Low calories. Low sex. Low speed—anorexic society. Curiously, in this world (America) where everything is available in profusion, everything has to be saved and economized.

Smile and others will smile back. Smile to show how transparent, how candid you are. Smile if you have nothing to say. Most of all, do not hide the fact you have nothing to say nor your total indifference to others. Let this emptiness, this profound indifference shine out spontaneously in your smile. *Give* your emptiness and indifference to others, light up your face with the zero degree of joy and pleasure, smile, smile, smile . . . Americans may have no identity, but they do have wonderful teeth.

—Jean Baudrillard, *America*[1]

Of pluralism, constitutionalism, and capitalism, the three root causes of trouble with America, it is capitalism which is most fundamental. Historically, it was capitalism which *caused* the emergence of pluralism and constitutionalism[2] and it is the prevalence of pro-capitalist sentiments in this country which *continues* to promote and support the unhealthy belief in pluralism and constitutionalism as political ideals. There should be a little mystery about capitalism's relationship to pluralism and constitutionalism. The principal point of pluralism, the dispersal of power, is to render government too weak to pose much of a threat to the wealthy and their property. Similarly, the primary point of constitutionalism, the limitation of government power, is to keep government too contained to threaten the wealthy and their property. As we saw in the preceding two chapters, a government condemned to perpetual gridlock may not feature control by the rich but it does guarantee that there will be little change to upset their privilege. A government contained by constitutional restraints, especially when those constraints are better defined and more rigorously applied concerning property rights than other rights such as speech rights is one that well protects the position of the upper classes. Here then is a very sad and troubling truth about American political values: both of our core abstract notions about political virtue, both pluralist and constitutionalist sentiments, are really present and prevalent because they tend to yield as an outcome weak and restrained government that suits the rich and the status quo. Perhaps then it is our core abstract notion about economic virtue, our society's nearly mindless faith in capitalism, which lies closest to the ultimate heart of the reason for all the trouble with America.

In this country, faith in capitalism may be roughly akin to a religious fervor. It has its own detailed dogma of beliefs—articles of faith *not* particularly well grounded in fact. Among the central tenets of capitalist belief are the notions that capitalism is a system of free enterprise, open to all; that it rewards talent, hard work, and luck (and that those who benefit most under it are those who have the largest combination of these three assets although any one of the three may be sufficient to guarantee success); and that it is the most efficient way in which to structure an economy because it responds best to the demands of consumers, the law of supply and demand that sets prices and encourages investments in the most efficient way practicable. In many ways, it is a fine religion. The trouble is that there is very little truth to these beliefs.

Far from being an economy of free enterprise open to all, the American economy ensures that *viable* new business ventures are only available to those who can amass very large sums of money with which to invest, something far beyond the means of the vast majority of Americans. Sadly, very small-scale ventures are well known to be the most risky, with the overwhelming majority resulting in losses. Sadly, too, talent and hard work are not well correlated with economic success in America. Luck is somewhat of a better predictor of success, but for poor people to end up wealthy here, it needs to be quite copious amounts of luck (for example, winning a lottery despite the fact that your odds of being struck by lightning are considerably better). The typical hyper-rich American does not rank very highly in talent or industriousness. Instead, he or she (far more often he) was, on average, a C student in college, far below the now average college grade of B, and his only major piece of good fortune was being born into a position of wealth, a position of privilege which alone is the best predictor of future financial gains in America.[3] As for hard work, those who work the longest hours and who have the most back breaking chores (for example, digging ditches, moving furniture, and loading cargo) are heavily concentrated in the *lowest* paying occupations.

So, does capitalism at least live up to its mythology when it comes to efficiency? Is the prospect of making more money the best inducement to creativity and effort? Does the "law" of supply and demand efficiently set prices and provide incentive for new investment whenever and wherever it is needed? No. Not really. The literature on productivity is fairly clear in finding that the promise of more money is *not* a very good inducement of increased productivity. Instead, workers who have more pleasant working conditions such as a cheerful work atmosphere, good lighting, time for socializing, some control over the work pace and process greatly outperform those who are merely offered more money for higher output. Indeed, the promise of more money seems to have a dampening effect on productivity because it seems to suggest that the chore at hand is so unpleasant, so internally unrewarding, that one must be offered significant increments in external motivation (in other words, more money) to be induced to do it. Economists and business administrators have known this for years and capitalists have reveled in the upshot, namely, that the best productivity gains can be earned with relatively inexpensive adjustments in the work environment rather than with expensive profit minimizing raises for workers.[4]

As for prices of goods and services, wage levels for various occupations, and the decision matrices governing investment patterns, these things are not governed by supply and demand so much as they simply reflect *power* related variables such as control (and the desire of elites to try to keep what economic control they may have), status (heavily influenced by class, race, and gender), and prejudice (which typically judges what people are worth and what they deserve quite apart from any objective measure of what they contribute). Consider just a few obvious examples. Truck drivers, overwhelmingly male, are rarely in short supply, but make far more money than most nurses, often in relatively short supply but, much to the detriment of their wages, preponderantly female.[5] Qualified candidates for the position of Chief Executive Officer (CEO) are hardly in shorter supply these days. However, since 1980, overall growth in both gross domestic product and corporate profits has been lackluster and yet average annual CEO salaries have increased from $625,000 to about $10 million. That's an increase of roughly 1,150 percent or over 600 percent controlling for inflation.[6] America's corporate elites have been getting richer much faster than America's corporations. Oil prices rise in part with steep increases in global demand but maybe even more so because of the increased power of the oligopolies (that is, an entire industry owned and controlled by a handful of companies) that set prices while keenly aware of the demand *in*elasticity of oil. In other words, oligopolistic oil companies can choose to set prices artificially high, far beyond what supply and demand factors would warrant, and they can be certain that consumption rates will not change very much. After all, what is the alternative to driving to work and heating one's home? In Europe and elsewhere, the alternative to driving may involve a competent mass transit system which, in most of America, simply does not exist and, no matter how high oil prices get here, we do not hear the clarion call for the creation of first-rate mass transit systems for virtually all of our cities.

Severely undermining capitalist "efficiency" are its massive problems of fraud, corporate welfare, and economic externalities. American capitalism suffers from enormous loss and waste due to malfeasance and theft, probably because there may be little functional difference between unmitigated greed, the engine that drives capitalism, carried on within the confines of lawful behavior and unmitigated greed that occasionally exceeds those bounds. In any case, even though, unlike public sector fraud and waste, private sector malfeasance is far more likely to be covered up and its costs simply passed on to consumers, the scope of this inefficiency of greed is obvious. Consider the magnitude of just the two best-known instances of massive corporate crime: the Savings and Loan scandal of the 1980s and the Enron scandal of 2001. The Savings and Loan scandal involved a banking equivalent of a pyramid scheme. Bank owners and bank officials illegally tapped into their institutions' assets to make new investments (typically new loans and deposit brokerages which are commissions for finding the highest certificate of deposit rates). As the malfeasance eventually became widely known and as more and more banks began to teeter and fail, the federal government stepped in with bailouts totaling over $125 billion, which at the time was nearly $500 for *every* American woman, man, and child. The Enron scandal was, in essence, an accounting fraud in which Enron executives lied about company profits and hid debts and losses so that they could unload their shares in the company at about $90 per share before the value collapsed to pennies a share. This left other investors and mostly the company's workers who had their entire retirement funds in Enron stock to suffer the consequences of collapsing stock values. All told, the losses amounted to more than $60 billion.

Massive corporate welfare is another telltale sign of capitalism's inefficiency. Corporate welfare refers to corporations' receipt of often-huge government subsidies to help support the business. Sometimes the purported goal is to keep certain businesses from failing or relocating or to encourage environmental cleanups, but often it is just to prop up profits. Just as the cost of tax breaks for interest paid on mortgages by middle and upper class homeowners dwarfs the money government spends on housing subsidies for the poor, so here the costs of welfare for corporations dwarfs the amount spent on welfare for the poor. There are hosts of inefficiencies here. For example, in New York State, a brownfields cleanup subsidy program not only pays back corporations for the cost of buying and cleaning up contaminated sites, it also pays the full cost of whatever new enterprise is placed on that site.[7] As a result, corporations have rushed to buy contaminated old gas stations and to build high rise hotels there as a means of getting a "free" hotel. In other instances, New York State officials are finding that companies that have accepted cleanup subsidies have done little or nothing to actually clean up the sites.

All too typically, of course, the reason for the offending contaminations has been the behavior of corporations in the first place. Under capitalist conditions, companies can impose huge costs on the rest of society by polluting, among other things. These economic externalities are not part of their calculations of the profitability of their activities because it will typically be government and society (not them) that will have to pay the costs of either enduring with an unpleasant or even deadly environment or of the need to clean up the mess. Some may object that it is *government's* obligation to protect society with regulatory legislation but, as we have already seen, pluralist government is *by design* too weak to perform this function with any reliability. Different types of economies likewise can be ecologically irresponsible. However, when corporations can benefit from activities that elicit more harm than benefit because they get all or most of the benefit but leave to others all or most of the harm, environmental irresponsibility becomes profitable, encouraged, and a much bigger problem than it would be in a society with a more powerful government that either issues meaningful protective legislation or directly manages development projects with significant environmental impact potential. As a result, toxic dumping, low efficiency smokestacks, strip mining, and the like have become ubiquitous problems in America. Of course, with all its copious signage, neon and otherwise, and billboards, video and conventional, American capitalist huckstering is just plain ugly even when aesthetic appeal is the only fatality.

But even apart from the ugliness and waste that comes from a capitalism relatively unregulated by competent government, the pricing practices of capitalism reveal perhaps an even deeper inefficiency. Under capitalism, each and every time a product changes hands—from manufacturer to distributor, from distributor to wholesaler, from wholesaler to retailer, and finally from retailer to consumer—the price of the product roughly doubles or more. Unless this is efficiency in fleecing customers, it is hard to know what kind of core "efficiency" is at work here.

What is this capitalism of ours, if not as described in far too many of our uncritical textbooks, the "efficient" "free enterprise" system where, thankfully, individuals and not government own most business and property? Capitalism is more accurately described as an economic system in which the overwhelming majority of resource is owned and controlled privately and the distribution of income and wealth tends to be highly unequal. That most resource is owned and controlled privately is *not* to say that the economic system is particularly free, open, or individualistic. Indeed, the depressing reality of ownership in America is such that only 1 percent of Americans own roughly 40 percent of all the wealth[8] and the vast majority of American individuals have little hope of ever possessing any opportunity to meaningfully partake in this "free" and "open" system. It is true that capitalism has no completely inevitable distribution outcome. It is theoretically possible that we could all compete in a capitalist economy and somehow all end up with exactly equal shares. Of course, this is only a theoretical possibility and a very remote one at that. Instead, the general nature of capitalist practice seems to reward having large sums to invest, far more than it rewards creativity or enterprise, and so, over time, it tends to make the rich richer and to keep the poor at bay.

In capitalism, it is both ownership and control of businesses that must be in private hands. If ownership alone is privatized but control is firmly in the public domain with either massive regulation or, more significantly, very progressive taxation, then there is every possibility that government will implement a tax code that is so progressive that it redistributes wealth from the rich to the poor such that meaningful inequalities are severely restricted. Sweden is such a case in point. Nearly all resource is owned privately but the 90 percent plus tax rates on the rich create a more equalitarian order that is unmistakably socialist.

Of all the developed capitalist countries of the world, there is none more extreme or untempered in its capitalism than the United States. This is evident in several ways. First, the gulf between rich and poor is wider in the United States than in any other developed capitalist country. Second, the United States, being such a young nation, as compared, for example, to our European counterparts, has no significant pre-capitalist history or traditions to be influenced by, to temper, or to alter the impact of our capitalistic impulses. Here there are no significant traditions of ruling Church or monarchy, no bygone era of a feudal order under which notions of national identity slowly fought their way into being. Instead, our founding philosophies are all relatively blatant in their capitalist ethos of acquisition. Consider the

What is the Alternative to Capitalism? Socialism

There have been many kinds of pre-capitalist economies; slave economies, feudal economies, and mercantilist economies (wherein the old aristocratic class left over from feudal days imposes high taxes and regulations on entrepreneurs to siphon off much of the wealth) are the principal examples. In fascist societies, a variation on capitalism, corporativism, has the defining feature of allowing interference with "free market" principles but primarily in order to direct investment toward military production and to keep the prices of military production relatively affordable to the fascist state. However, in the contemporary world, the primary alternative to capitalism is socialism.

Socialism is an economic system in which the majority of resource is owned *or* controlled publicly and the distribution of income and wealth tends to be relatively equal. Notice from this definition that, in socialism, the public pre-eminence in economics can come from either government ownership (as is generally the primary method of public pre-eminence in communist states) *or* various means of governmental control (for example, intensive and extensive regulation of business but, most especially, heavily progressive taxation which redistributes income and wealth away from the rich and toward the middle and lower classes, as is typically the case in most socialist parliamentary polities). Both government ownership of most businesses and heavily progressive taxation of income and/or wealth tend to produce a much more equal distribution of money and resource than capitalism does. Autogestion, the ownership of businesses by their workers, is also associated with socialist economies and tends to produce more equal distributions of resource (because the workers generally have equal shares in the business) but it is not widely used.

There is no such thing as a purely equalitarian order in which everyone owns exactly the same amount but, generally speaking, communist societies (at least when non-corrupted) impose the greatest degrees of equality whereas socialist polities are typically content with abolishing the extremes of wealth and poverty characteristic of capitalism. This then is the virtue of socialist economies: they take as an ideal the goals of eliminating poverty and of creating a greater societal cohesiveness—less pluralism, in essence—by mitigating or even eliminating social class distinctions. The goal of attaining a social order in which *everyone* is well fed, is well clothed, has quality health care, has extensive education, and has the assurance of a good job and a good income—these are the hallmark qualities of socialist economics. Capitalists have a hard time believing that such an economy can adequately motivate people to work hard but, as we have already seen, productivity research suggests that monetary rewards are poor motivators of workers. Instead, a happy, healthy, and social workforce is a much more productive one. The very aberrational person who might refuse to work in a socialist economy could face ostracism and other social sanctions. However, socialism, unlike capitalism, generally does not use the threat of poverty as an agent of societal control.

following foundational philosophies in relation to how each promotes capitalism:

- Smithian economics from a zealous exaggeration of Adam Smith's 1776 *The Wealth of Nations*: the assertion being that, under capitalism, from private vice (the selfish desire for purely personal gain) inadvertently emerges the public good (everyone benefits, everyone gains resource, albeit not equally). This is an application of the famous "invisible hand" analogy: no one plans or intends the public well-being; it is an inadvertent outcome of a society organized upon principles of laissez-faire economics (that is, minimal regulation of business) in which so many individuals are supposedly so active and imaginative in their pursuit of private gain that everyone, even the least effortful and creative, is thought to gain.[9] Sadly, even in 1776, this argument was no longer accurate. It seems to aptly describe only the very earliest phases of capitalism and even by 1776, in Britain and America, the rich were getting richer primarily at the expense of the poor and *not* to the benefit of all.
- Madisonian pluralism, which, as we saw in chapter 1, lifts the Smithian argument and applies it to the governmental realm. Again, private vice (engaging in politics solely in the pursuit of personal gain) is encouraged as a supposed means of inadvertently delivering the public good (a political environment in which all are stalemated, incapable of making significant personal gains at the expense of others because there are so many incompatible others trying to do the same thing).
- Lockean constitutionalism, which argues that the entire need for government arises from the invention of money and the more significant inequalities it allows. The need for government, in John Locke's view, is to protect private property. Government can and should be restricted to the general task of private property protection.

All three of these bedrock theories upon which American government and society rest celebrate and defend one thing not normally considered a virtue: greed. Critics of capitalism may be quick to point out that greed is, in fact, no virtue; that, in Smithian America, the rich get richer as the poor stagnate or even get poorer; that, in Madisonian America, gridlock protects the status quo which confers privilege on the rich and underprivilege on the poor; that, in Lockean America, protection of private property alone fails to adequately address the needs of typical Americans hoping for a richer life, hoping for some viable means of amassing property significant enough to be worthy of protection. Still, all this may be missing the deeper point. With capitalism and greed at the root of our social and political culture, there is something perverse and even vacuous about American "culture."

At the center of American political "culture," if there is such a thing as a culture in America, is a nearly ubiquitous belief in the American dream: a faith that, in the United States, all who work hard are likely to be rewarded with a nice house, a spouse, a car, 1.5 children (more or less), and perhaps even an annual vacation or two. Those who combine hard work with a little bit of, or a lot of, talent and/or luck, can expect to achieve all this more readily and perhaps to achieve much more of this (for example, an even bigger and nicer house, a fancier car, etc.). At the heart of this "culture," is a very strange belief that those who "are better," in other words, those who have the most talent to expedite their acquisitions, deserve to be wealthier. It is unclear why. It would be just as logical to expect that those who have the greatest natural talents should be able to live as well as their less talented peers with *less* rather than more because they could use their extra skills to be cleverer and more efficient in their consumption practices. But the American dream is hardly egalitarian. Instead, it calls for the most talented to enjoy added riches along with their added abilities. One might guess that the purpose of pampering the most able is to encourage them to contribute more to the greater good. If the most able are happier, they may be more inclined to create those new inventions or undertake those new initiatives that might benefit many around them. Of course, such an idea may contradict the false assumptions about motivation and productivity that underlie capitalism insofar as the rich may soon attain a level of comfort that *dampens* their urge to struggle for still more. Oddly, the American dream seems to suggest that Americans, including the most talented, need not have any sense of civic or public duty but rather that the only impulse needed to guide their behavior is acquisitiveness.

But if the American dream entails no sense of civic or community responsibility and no obligation to charity, neither does it seem realistic or accurate when measured against the actual patterns of American social class immobility and lack of opportunity. Long-term longitudinal studies of social class mobility in first world countries suggest that the United States has the poorest/lowest economic mobility, both within a lifetime and across generations. This is especially true for both the earnings mobility of low paid workers and for the exit rates from poverty (i.e., the rates at which the poor manage to escape poverty and join the ranks of better paid employees).[10] America may be a place where it is easiest for the rich to get richer (especially over the past few decades, not because of any large productivity gains but rather because of significant reductions in real tax rates on the wealthy), but it is most certainly *not* a place where there is relatively good opportunity for the mobility of the poor and middle classes. European nations uniformly score much higher in these regards, most likely because the much more generous programs in public health, education, and welfare all seem very useful, if not absolutely necessary, for promoting economic mobility among the lower classes. It is only when basic needs are met and when there is security—freedom from the economic stresses that can come from injury, illness, or high tuition—that the poor are best able to plan for, and achieve, economic mobility.

It is generally the more privileged of Americans who know little about capitalism's effects upon ordinary people who can afford to be enthusiastic about our economy. For example, using 2005 data, it is still the richest one-fifth of Americans, those who have annual family incomes above $103,100, who constitute the overwhelming bulk of the less than one-quarter of Americans who complete a four year college degree. The poorest one-fifth of Americans have combined annual incomes below $25,617 and, as a result, little opportunity to do much of anything other than subsist. With a median family income of $54,061, America is not nearly as rich or as elite as many Americans suppose. It is also critically important to realize that the rich have most certainly been getting relatively richer and the poor relatively poorer. Since 1947, the income of the upper fifth has jumped from 43 percent of all income to now more than 48 percent of all income while, for every other quintile, the proportion of total national income has fallen roughly proportionally, a drop of about one and one-quarter percent of national income for each group. The poorest fifth of Americans now live on merely 4 percent of total national income. The wealthiest 1 percent, with annual incomes (in 2005) above $348,000, have more than 22 percent of the nation's total income—the most top heavy distribution of income we have seen since the late 1920s, just before the stock market crash ushered in the Great Depression.[11] The wealthiest one-hundredth of a percent of the population have (again using 2005 data) annual family incomes above $5 million and more than 5 percent of the nation's total income, also higher than at any time since the late 1920s.[12] Inequalities in *wealth* (rather than income) reflect many years of disparate income levels and are thus far more unequal. The wealthiest one-fifth of Americans now own more than 80 percent of the country's wealth.[13] In sum, over time capitalism works better and better for America's rich but it is incredibly harmful and unfair to most everyone else.

Americans almost certainly work harder than ever before. As more of the U.S. economy has been redistributed from the lower and middle classes to the wealthy, middle class Americans have generally taken on longer hours and extra jobs as a means of keeping roughly the same standard of living available to their families several decades ago.[14] Has the American dream of a land where anyone can make it, to be successful and affluent, become merely a cover for a reality in which the rich get richer (through increasing tax breaks) while the middle class works harder and harder just to tread water and the poor work harder and harder just to scrape by? In such an America, where credit card companies encourage massive indebtedness and jack up interest rates to about 30 percent for all who fail to keep up with payments and where mortgage companies specialize in low tease rates only to jack up interest rates several fold for those who fall behind—what is this if not the new indentured servitude? In such an America, where the majority will never be able to accumulate sufficient assets to begin a viable capitalist enterprise and will have no option other than to lease themselves by the hour, usually at depressingly low wages, what is this if not the new slavery wherein the "slaves" are leased rather than owned outright? When the poor have no means to subsist other than by renting themselves out by the hour for very low wages, we have not really moved very far from an economy in which they were owned outright or mortgaged themselves for many months.

Quite apart from the effects of any "new slavery," the U.S. economy is still feeling the effects of the "old" slavery and it is at the intersection of capitalism and race in America that economic bias is most pernicious. While formal and legal slavery ended in America roughly 150 years ago, it is still worth noting that this represents only about two full lifespans. Slavery was also far more savage than most white Americans realize. Where the crop was sugar, which required prompt and rapid cane cutting and even more hurried cane processing, African slaves had a lifespan of months, not years, and were intentionally worked to death as a necessary cost of the business. The toll claimed the lives of millions of slaves, making the slaving of Africans perhaps the largest genocide in human history. While sugar production was far less prevalent in North America than in the Caribbean and South America, here the importation and breeding of slaves became part of a rape culture in which slave owners horrifically abused their slaves and, to minimize rebellion, worked hard to dismantle African cultures, to keep slaves separate from their countrymen and countrywomen, to prohibit literacy and schooling, and so on.

The subsequent eras of Klan hegemony, lynching, Jim Crow, and segregation (both the de jure segregation of the recent past and the de facto and residential segregation that endures) all meant that there could be little opportunity for African Americans. For nearly a century after slavery formally ended, fabricated charges and inappropriate convictions forced tens of thousands of African Americans into brutal convict labor.[15] To this day, the illegal status of many immigrants renders them subject to virtual slavery. Nor are such fairly recent activities like Klanism and Jim Crow even now entirely a thing of the past. More than half of white Americans hold blatantly racist beliefs (viewing blacks as innately lazy and less intelligent than whites); only 14 percent of available jobs appear in classifieds, which thus renders personal connections the key to employment and advancement in what is still a white dominated and racist society; and home lending biases and the racist attitudes of white home buyers who perceive the presence of blacks within a neighborhood as evidence of the neighborhood's undesirability, together make housing costs about 25 percent lower in white neighborhoods than they would be if the residents were black.[16] As George Lipsitz put it, "minorities are told in essence, 'We can't give you a loan today because we've discriminated against your race so effectively in the past that you have not been able to accumulate any equity from housing and to pass it down through the generations.'"[17]

It should not be surprising that, for many African Americans, economic disenfranchisement is accompanied by, and facilitated by, political disenfranchisement. A blatant example of this is the use of felon exclusion laws in most states. Mississippi may be the most extreme in doing what is widespread in America, that which has permanently disenfranchised 13 percent of African American men nationwide. There, false or trumped up felony charges are brought against huge numbers of African Americans who are then assured that their sentences will be suspended (i.e., no jail time) if they cop a plea. The only thing lost, and permanently at that, is their right to vote. In this manner, nearly one-third of Mississippi's black men have been permanently disenfranchised. In seven other states, more than one-quarter of black men have been permanently disenfranchised.[18] More alarming still may be the fact that this deplorable and blatantly racist practice is not even an issue in mainstream America which remains, by and large, perhaps somewhat willfully unaware of it.

Like racial minorities, women in America have been subjected to obvious discrimination in our capitalist economy. Women even now make little more than 70 cents on the dollar compared to their male peers of equal or lesser qualification. Apologists for unequal pay argue that women are more likely to miss work, interrupt careers, or even simply quit because of childcare and family issues. While this is true, women nonetheless have overall lower rates of absenteeism and resignation than their male counterparts. Women remain less likely to be promoted to the middle and upper levels of employment, trapped as they are beneath a "glass ceiling" that is still quite real and powerful. Gender based pay discrimination has been so obvious that a handful of states have enacted comparable worth laws to govern the payment of public employees. Those states have attempted to objectively measure the true "worth" of employees based on assessments of level of education necessary, difficulty of work, effort, and other such categories. The extension of such legislation into the private sector would require the abolition of the capitalist principles of pay determination and, while that is not about to happen anytime soon, the ways in which such plans have dramatically reduced gender bias in public sector pay in the few states where it has been used, strongly evidences how extensive a problem this is, how economically costly to women the relatively unregulated sexism of capitalism in America really is.

America certainly has its struggles with economic fairness as suggested by all of the above problems—classism as evident in both a lack of mobility and a lack of opportunity, racism, and sexism—but maybe what is most deplorable about capitalism in America is its vacuousness. A celebration of greed is not a substantive notion of what is good. Americans may know that they want more, but they have little sense of what values they should hold and little awareness that values are generally not attained via consumer purchases. In short, an ethos of greed is not much of an ethos. Perhaps a generation or two ago, Americans had some inkling of this but it seems relatively absent from modern America. Consider, for example, the famous 1948 film *Key Largo*. Humphrey Bogart played Frank McCloud, a World War II veteran who goes to Key Largo to visit the father (Mr. Temple) and widow (Nora Temple) of a fallen comrade. Frank eventually has to overcome his new pacifist impulses *and* his lingering fears to defend himself and, more importantly, others from the ravages of the newly arrived evil gangster Johnny Rocco, played by Edward G. Robinson. Before the decisive gun play where good triumphs over evil at the end of the movie, the dramatic confrontation between the two men unfolds as follows:

Johnny: He's got a gun, you think, and I haven't. You figure it's the gun. Well, listen, soldier. Thousands of guys got guns but there's only one Johnny Rocco.

Mr. Temple: How do you account for it?

Frank: Well, he knows what he wants. Don't you, Rocco?

Johnny: Sure.

Mr. Temple: What's that?

Frank: Tell him, Rocco.

Johnny: (unsure) Well, I want . . . uh . . .

Frank: He wants more. Don't you, Rocco?

Johnny: (excited) Yeah, that's it! More. That's right. I want more!

Mr. Temple: Will you ever get enough?

Frank: Will you, Rocco?

Johnny: Well, I never have. No, I guess I won't.

In 1948, that exchange of words told moviegoers that Johnny Rocco was evil—evil because he had an endless desire for more. Is it possible that only sixty years later Smithian economics and the new conservatism have taken such hold in America that we all aspire *to be* little Johnny Roccos? Not necessarily with a willingness to resort to racketeering and murder to get ahead but at least insofar as we are encouraged to have an endless desire for more and to not think anything is evil about that impulse?

However, over the past several decades, real annual growth in America has been, at best, only about half of what it was in the 1950s, '60s, and '70s and so most of us feel remarkably limited in our ability to get more. At the same time, we are scheming and planning, working, studying, and investing (even if only in ourselves), we are typically scrimping and saving—in short, *minimizing* our contributions to others. It is this point that Baudrillard makes in the quotation with which we began this chapter. America has become an obsessional, phobic, and anorexic society, a land where, despite the relative affluence, everything is to be saved and economized. But Baudrillard could have been far more critical with his choice of words and examples. For example, while we Americans love money, relatively speaking, we don't particularly love good food. Instead, we dine too often on the nearly indigestible "food" served at many fast food joints, and we eat a plethora of overly salty, excessively sugared, heavy indelicate, and/or frozen and then warmed foods at any number of the chain restaurants that currently dominate the American eatery scene. Relatively speaking, we do not appear to love learning. Rather, we tend to look for things we can pretend are quick fixes and read the latest "Idiot's Guide" to this or that. Relatively speaking, we have no love of art or literature. Instead, even if we are not permanently plugged into television where the same five or six story lines are played out again and again in whatever mindless crime story is on at the moment, our best seller lists feature almost entirely murder and spy "thrillers" in which the same few plot lines are redrawn with slightly new nuances time and time again. In books or on television, these ubiquitous "thrillers" may be America's propaganda. These simplistic tales of "good" versus "evil" told principally from the vantage point of police (in crime stories) or government (in spy stories) may be intended to distract people from *real* everyday politics, the politics of economic distribution in America, and its consequences. Sadly, building our culture around profit maximization appears to undermine rather than enhance our taste in food, knowledge, art, and entertainment.

Here perhaps is where American capitalism has failed most of us most powerfully: it has taught us a good bit about more but, by failing to offer us anything beyond greed as our goal, it teaches us precious little about good. And maybe that's intentional. After all, the point of capitalism is to sell people the cheap crap you have to sell, not the things that are necessarily good for them. It is a lie to suggest that the American economy is driven by the demands of consumers, free to insist upon the goods and services they desire and demand. Instead, capitalism is driven by profit maximization, something best attained by convincing consumers, largely through ever present ads, to desire the *cheap* goods and services which, despite high profit margins, allow consumers to afford more of them in lieu of quality products that might truly nourish the body and soul. Of course, bad taste can be cultivated and American businesses have worked diligently and successfully in cultivating just that in a majority of Americans. Certainly, American consumers have "choices" to make but all too often these are false choices (for example, to consume something TV ads have told me I should want *or* take my chances with something unknown; or to buy my warmed frozen food from *this* chain or *that* one) and they are made without adequate information (what's in this? how much does it cost to produce and how much profit is being taken? how many and which of these stores are ultimately the same, that is, owned by the same company?).

Baudrillard's most stinging critique and his most compelling argument is that we Americans have no identity. We smile often and easily but it is a kind of killer smile that we offer instead of saying something of substance. Thoroughly immersed in our ethos of "more for me," we are not interested enough in others to have much to say to them. And we smile through beautiful teeth because those of us who are at all successful have been well taught to purchase that which appeals to our sense of vanity. Dentistry will always do well in a narcissistic society. Vanity and insecurity, like bad taste, are perhaps inevitable epidemics in capitalist economies. Capitalists are driven by the urge to sell more products and few strategies for doing so are more effective than massive advertising designed to make people feel that they are undesirable and unattractive without a slew of products to cover up their many "defects" and enhance their "assets." A truly secure population might find solace in themselves and each other, would probably not buy as much, not seek makeovers, not look for distraction from poor self-image and lack of friends in consumerism, and, God forbid, they might actually build up their savings accounts. It is not true that they would simply buy as much of other things. Besides, the key to capitalism's best profits is selling cheap things at high prices. "Beauty" products and chain restaurant frozen food are just two key examples of product lines particularly well suited to that goal.

Despite the nice teeth, all the chain restaurant food, years upon years of television viewing, and gads of cheap things to purchase, identitylessness is no bargain. Capitalism's greatest flaw may be that it poses an impediment to the development of substantive moral and social visions of the good life and, in so doing, actively undermines our individual and collective human development. But no worries. If we become depressed by these realities, we can help pharmaceutical companies maximize their profits by buying lots and lots of overpriced anti-depressants. That so many Americans are mired in the use and abuse of alcohol and drugs, legal and not, powerfully suggests that there is something seriously deficient with the ethos of greed. Americans would be far better served with a substantive cultural identity, something far better rooted in values pertaining to history, custom, food, ideology, intellectual pursuits, religion, art, literature, and/or music. "We want more," however, is no proper functional identity.

The most famous critic of capitalism, Karl Marx, was keenly aware of capitalism's tendency to destroy genuine social identities and to replace them with an unhealthy "fetishism of commodities."[19] In the United States, we have capitalism without any significant pre-capitalist phase of economic development and hence, never having held any truly substantive identity earlier, the trouble with identity can be expected to be especially onerous in America. Marx's critique of capitalism's fetishism of commodities suggests that capitalism creates an unhealthy and perverse enthusiasm for consumer goods, a kind of crass materialism that excessively focuses upon products and simultaneously entails an *under*-appreciation for the social relationships among humans. In other words, we now seek happiness and excitement in high definition televisions, iPods, digital video recorders, and the like precisely as we are progressively cut off more and more from one another. In previous generations, there was extraordinary excitement over home ownership, so much so that one could almost envision new homeowners endlessly admiring if not fondling or caressing the staircase banister or some other fine appointment of a home. That may be less likely to occur with the latest generation of Americans. Because they are a tad wealthier and often take more wealth as a given, they may save their drooling for other things: sex (sadly and perversely conceptualized as a good for consumption rather than part of a deep and romantic relationship), alcohol and drugs (not so much a social activity as an escape from others and perhaps even from oneself), or maybe an exotic vacation or two. The fetishism isn't new; only the objects, to which it is attached, take on new fashions. Sadly, in contemporary America, shopping has become conceptualized not as the means to an end, getting what one needs or wants, but rather as itself a form of entertainment, often the only readily available or seemingly "affordable" "entertainment."

Related to Marx's concern about crass materialism was his fear of the alienation of labor—one of capitalism's most dehumanizing effects.[20] This unhappy condition caused by capitalism has several components:

- An alienation from the work process such that what was once rewarding, emotionally fulfilling, and skill enhancing labor becomes dehumanizing, repetitive, mind numbing, and soul depleting work.
- An alienation from our human nature because, according to Marx, it is our basic nature to be productive and, if meaningful labor is replaced with dehumanizing work, we will lose touch with ourselves, our own best qualities, and our true potential.

- Alienation from the product. Marx makes a key point here: it is the working class that makes everything but they don't get to keep the products of their labors. Instead, capitalists, who produce nothing themselves, push around paper, manipulate investments amidst an economic order that allows them to appropriate the overwhelming bulk of the profits emanating from production. In other words, capitalists pay laborers far less than the market price of the laborers' products, take these products away from their true producers to whom they rightfully belong, and sell the goods at market, pocketing huge profits. By its very nature, capitalism is exploitive.
- Alienation from sociality. This means that a non-exploitive economic order would allow workers every opportunity for meaningful and enriching social interactions with other workers but what typically happens, under capitalism, is a separation of workers one from another, as much caused by the desire to keep the working class repressed as it is by the effects of a very crude form of mechanization.

Taken together, these various kinds of alienation make for a very unhappy population, who may nonetheless remain largely mystified about the relationship between capitalism and their unhappiness. It may be useful to think of this in a somewhat different way: capitalism may be devoid of any specific cultural identity or cultural content other than acquisitiveness or greed itself and the strange notions that come with it. It is fueled by a belief that more is better and a belief that the stuff that capitalists can sell at a healthy profit is the stuff that we should want and that can facilitate our happiness. And yet, while capitalism has a vacuous and even insipid *"cultural"* content, it most certainly has a substantive *method*. At the heart of that method is competition.

It is true that, at times, capitalism can fail to live up to its method as, for example, when monopolies emerge or, more commonly, when a handful of companies (an oligopoly) conspires to dominate a particular market by refusing to compete with one another. However, especially at the middle and lower levels of businesses and individuals, capitalism is a system of hypercompetitiveness. Mid-size and small businesses must constantly struggle against one another and against bigger companies which are typically eager to take over larger and larger segments of the economy. And it is not just individual entrepreneurs who compete tooth and nail against each other but also employees looking for better jobs and promotions and students competing for better grades and board scores to get into the better academic programs to get the better jobs and so on. Americans are always competing against one another, so much so that even our "recreation" and "entertainment" focuses on competitive activities. It is nearly impossible to imagine

Americans playing sports the way some Native American nations did: playing for hours upon hours as effortfully as possible but with an understanding that no one should ever keep score. In America we insist upon winners and losers—winners and losers in "reality" television, winners and losers in school, winners and losers in the economy, winners and losers in life.

Apologists for capitalism argue that all this competition is a good thing. It keeps us on our toes they say; it makes for an efficient economy by eliciting our best efforts. Of course there is no evidence that it does any of that. Rather, there is much reason to believe that hyper-competitiveness makes many of us give up trying. After all, losing is no fun. What's missing in America because of capitalism is a sense of play, a joie de vivre in which the activity itself is joyful quite apart from some strange and artificial notion of its "outcome." It may be "un-American" to suggest that the true "winners" are those who had fun but it also is far more sensical than keeping score of who performed "best."

What America loses with its hyper-competitive capitalist economy is community—in other words, an environment of friendliness, cooperation, and sociality. What kind of teamwork, what kind of cooperation can we expect from people in an environment where few are rewarded, generally for beating their peers? The most competitive of our academic institutions, for example, are infamous for instances in which students steal or hide research materials needed by their classmate competitors. Is this a healthy or efficient society? Capitalists like to talk about economies of scale but what of economies of cooperation? Think of it: imagine American neighborhoods not where people rush to build bigger fences and wherein most everyone believes it is their job to take care of themselves, but rather one in which the strategy for making purchases and meeting needs is cooperative. In suburbia, for example, does it really make sense for each one-acre landowner to buy her or his own rider mower? Wouldn't it be more economical for the neighborhood to develop a common sense of identity and purpose, for each to pitch in toward the purchase and maintenance of one really good tractor? The costs per person would be much lower, the maintenance woes considerably fewer, and there would probably be enough savings for everyone to simply hire some youngster to do all the mowing in the neighborhood. In a sense, this is just an economy of scale from the other direction, one in consumer behavior rather than in manufacturing. But capitalism, with its hyper-competitive, anti-social ways, deplores economies of scale of this sort. Indeed, it generally makes them impossible.

This then is the legacy of capitalism in America: the most extreme gaps between rich and poor of any developed nation; incredible inequities based on class, race, and gender (not an equality of opportunity but instead opportunity for the privileged wealthy and the lowest rates of opportunity for the poor, minorities, and women); a crass materialism that actively undermines rather than fosters a substantive cultural identity; a "tasteless" society in which notions of quality are constantly dismantled in favor of quantity; and a hyper-competitive, unfriendly, and just plain wasteful and inefficient way of life that dehumanizes and disappoints. Strange as it may seem, it turns out that Johnny Rocco is not a particularly good role model after all.

NOTES

1. Jean Baudrillard, *America*, trans. Chris Turner (London: Verso, 1988), 40, 34.

2. If you have any doubts about this, take a look at John Locke's *Second Treatise of Government*. His whole case for a constitutional republic rests on what he considers the sanctity of property rights. John Locke, *Second Treatise of Government*, ed. C. B. Macpherson (Indianapolis: Hackett Publishing Co., 1980/1690).

3. It is well known that extreme wealth is not well correlated with intelligence or hard work. Instead, it is, by far, best correlated with birth into a privileged affluent family. See, for example, Chuck Collins, *Born on Third Base: The Sources of Wealth of the 1996 Forbes 400* (Boston: United for a Fair Economy, 1997), as cited in G. William Domhoff, *Who Rules America: Power and Politics*, 4th ed. (Boston: McGraw Hill, 2002), 57. Collins found that 70 percent of the Forbes 400 list for 1996 was born into extreme or considerable affluence. For more details about the lack of correlation between wealth and intelligence, see Jay L. Zagorsky, "Do You Have to be Smart to be Rich? The Impact of IQ on Wealth, Income and Financial Distress," *Intelligence* 35, no. 5 (September/October 2007): 489–501.

4. See, for example, Jim Collins, *Good to Great: Why Some Companies Make the Leap and Others Don't* (New York: Harper Business, 2001), 49–52; Edward E. Lawler III, *The Ultimate Advantage: Creating the High Involvement Organization* (San Francisco: Jossey-Bass Publishers, 1992); and David I. Levine and Laura.D'Andrea Tyson, "Participation, Productivity, and the Firm's Environment," in A. S. Blinder, ed., *Paying for Productivity: A Look at the Evidence* (Washington, D.C.: Brookings Institution, 1990), 183–243.

5. Unionization rates do *not* seem to be the key determinant of wages here. Nurses are now unionized at nearly the same rates as truck drivers, their educational requirements are far greater, hours comparable, but wages significantly lower.

6. John C. Bogle, *The Battle for the Soul of Capitalism* (New Haven: Yale University Press, 2005), 18.

7. It is estimated that New York State will lose up to one billion dollars to this corporate welfare boondoggle for the cleanup of just 54 sites, most of which would likely have been remediated without these excessive and unwarranted corporate tax breaks. For details, see Robert Moore, David Gahl, Tim Sweeney, and Jackson Morris, *Wasted Green: How Lost Revenue and State Spending Shortchange New York Taxpayers & the Environment* (Albany, NY: Environmental Advocates of New York, 2008), 6.

8. Lawrence Mishel, Jared Bernstein, and Sylvia Allegretto, *The State of Working America 2006/2007* (Ithaca, NY: ILR Press), 251.

9. Adam Smith never applied the phrase "invisible hand" in clear reference to capitalism. However, in his *The Theory of Moral Sentiments* of 1759, he wrote: "The

rich . . . in spite of their natural selfishness and rapacity, though they mean only their own conveniency . . . divide with the poor the produce of all of their improvements. They are led by an invisible hand to make nearly the same distribution of the necessaries of life, which would have been made, had the earth been divided into equal portions among its inhabitants." Cited in James Buchan, *The Authentic Adam Smith: His Life and Ideas* (New York: Norton, 2006), 63. Buchan concludes that this oblique reference is more religious than economic and that the "necessaries of life" refers to Stoic ease of body and peace of mind rather than economic shares.

10. Laurence Mishel, Jared Bernstein, and John Schmitt found that the United States had the lowest earnings mobility for low paid workers of eight countries studied, lagging far behind Finland, the United Kingdom, Italy, Denmark, Sweden, France, and Germany (see Lawrence Mishel, Jared Bernstein, and John Schmitt, *The State of Working America 2000/2001*, Ithaca, NY: ILR Press, 2001, 386). Markus Jäntti, Bernt Bratsberg, Kurt Röed, Oadbjörn Raaum, Robin Naylor, Eva Österbacka, Anders Björklund, and Tor Eriksson found that the United States ranks *last*, among the six countries they examined, in *inter*generational economic mobility out of the lowest quintile, lagging far behind Denmark, Finland, Norway, Sweden, and the United Kingdom. Cited in Mishel, Bernstein, and Allegretto, *State of Working America 2006/2007*, 102.

11. Mishel, Bernstein, and Allegretto, *State of Working America 2006/2007*, 59–60.

12. Louis Uchitte, "The Richest of the Rich, Proud of a New Guilded Age," *The New York Times*, July 15, 2007, 1, 20–21.

13. Mishel, Bernstein, and Allegretto, *State of Working America 2006/2007*, 252.

14. The average American now works about 15 percent longer than was the case about 25 years ago. This is caused largely (but not entirely) by dramatic increases in the paid work hours of American women, generally poorly paid, but typically making the difference between maintaining an earlier family standard of living or not. See Mishel, Bernstein, and Allegretto, *State of Working America 2006/2007*, 91.

15. See Douglas A. Blackmon, *Slavery by Another Name: The Re-Enslavement of Black Americans from the Civil War to World War II* (New York: Doubleday, 2008).

16. See George Lipsitz, *The Possessive Investment in Whiteness: How White People Profit from Identity Politics* (Philadelphia: Temple University Press, 1998), 1–23.

17. Lipsitz, *Investment in Whiteness*, 14.

18. See the landmark study, Jamie Fellner and Marc Mauer, "Losing the Vote: The Impact of Felon Disenfranchisement Laws in the United States," (Washington, D.C.: Human Rights Watch and The Sentencing Project, 1998).

19. For Marx's analysis of the fetishism of commodities and the alienation of labor, see Karl Marx, *The Economic and Philosophical Manuscripts of 1844* (Amherst, NY: Prometheus Books, 1988/1844).

20. Marx, *Economic and Philosophical Manuscripts*.

Part II

THE TROUBLE ITSELF

4

Making a Mess of Things at Home: The American Domestic Policy Environment

The United States is a great country *if* we take as greatness extraordinary military might—much like ancient Rome or Nazi Germany—capable of making a mark on the larger world, largely in the form of warring and pillaging. If, however, we see greatness as the creation of a healthy, happy, successful population well served by a wide range of domestic policies, then the United States is clearly *not* a great country. With one of the world's highest incomes and a treasure trove of resource, there is certainly enough means for greatness but, sadly, American government is so dysfunctional and American capitalism so effective in creating vast economic and social disparities that American society is, on balance, a failure. Indeed, if the United States was significantly poorer, our standards and expectations could be lower. In our case, however, success would entail a society in which virtually *everyone* is well fed, adequately clothed, decently housed, relatively safe, and has reasonably good health care, a good education, meaningful work and income, real opportunity for advancement, and a place within a vibrant culture. Societal success is reflected more in an ability to enhance the quality of life of one's own people than it is in any ability to deny quality of life to others through military conquests. Sadly, our distributions of resource and policy benefits are so unevenly and unfairly distributed that many less affluent countries, particularly those of Western Europe, come far closer to quality of life enhancing ideals than do we. Unlike much of Europe, the United States is a country with disturbingly large problems with poverty, crime, healthcare negligence, illiteracy and under-education, inopportunity, and cultural vacuity.

To make matters even worse, perhaps ours isn't even *a* country at all. Sharp divides in a land of hyper-competitiveness pit individual against individual, neighborhood against neighborhood, racial group against racial group, suburb against city, state against state, and red state against blue state. It has perhaps been a long time since there was last much oneness to our many. Furthermore, these divisions are as much the cause of additional problems as they are the reflection of previous ones. In America, it is the *structural* divide of federalism that prevents the kinds of policies we need most and exacerbates our unhealthy localist tendencies.

As we saw in the previous chapter, at the heart of American political culture lies a belief in greed. Greed, however, unfortunately leads to hypocrisy more than it promotes virtue. Individually, there is probably no shortage of Americans who are willing and eager to help the needy and who are surprisingly tolerant of differences. Collectively, however, we generate government policies that are among the stingiest in the developed world when it comes to poverty relief at home and non-military foreign aid internationally. Nor is there much of a public response to the disturbingly large expressions of racism in a country where racism has been a constant source of abuse, poverty, and repression.

Where are our leaders? Where are out great statesmen? Not those politicians who congratulate us on being great when we are in fact not, but those who inspire us to be better; where are they? America is not a place where such leadership is likely to emerge, and for many reasons. For one thing, our faith in representation leads to a political climate wherein our politicians try to *follow* pre-existing prejudice as much as or more than they try to lead, ironically undermining both genuine representation and leadership. For another thing, the role of money in the politics of a hyper-capitalist, pluralist, stagnant, and fragmented society is such that our best leaders are rarely privileged enough to be in contention for influence.

In the end, what Americans do best is to try to protect themselves: minimize taxes, minimize government, avoid public responsibility for one another, and eschew public solutions to our common problems in favor of private "solutions" that almost always turn out to be inadequate. The result is an America that views government as the problem rather than a potential tool for solving most of our problems; the result is a new form of anarchism in which social responsibility is abdicated, where human needs go increasingly unmet, and our social order increasingly unravels. No, this is not a great country. Rather, it is a bit of a mess.

THE REVERSE ROBIN HOOD: TAXING THE POOR AND FEEDING THE RICH

American capitalism generates huge inequalities, larger than those created by any other developed country. However, unlike comparable nations,

American tax policy does relatively little to mitigate those inequalities and, with disproportionately large amounts of regressive taxation in which the poorer pay higher rates than the richer, the problem is only exacerbated.

There are at least three obvious signs that something is severely wrong with the federal tax structure. First, the country's only significant progressive tax, one that applies generally higher rates upon the richer than the poorer—the income tax—is only anemically progressive. Never particularly progressive by European standards, where tax rates top 50 percent for the wealthiest and often reach 90 percent or more in socialist countries, the effective federal income tax rate on the richest 1 percent of Americans is, at this writing, about 27 percent. This is markedly lower than 37 percent, what the rate for the wealthiest 1 percent was in the 1970s. The bottom three-quarters of the richest one-fifth, the 80th through 95th percentile of the population, has an effective federal income tax rate of 22 percent, down from the 27.5 percent rate of the 1970s. For the middle classes, the second through fourth fifths of the income distribution, the effective tax rates range from 11 to 20 percent—not all that much lower, especially by the standards of the world's more civilized nations.[1] Champions of a new flat tax structure, which would impose roughly the same effective tax rate on everyone if ever implemented, would be making an anemically progressive income tax not at all progressive. Meanwhile, there is no significant movement here to create a tax system that is progressive by European standards.

The second obvious oddity and trouble sign is the relatively low percentage of total governmental revenue generated by the federal personal income tax. Only 42.5 percent of federal revenue and less than 28 percent of total governmental (federal, state *and* local) revenue is raised by our mildly progressive federal income tax. There are *other* minor and mildly progressive taxes in America: the federal corporate income tax (less than 14 percent of federal revenue; 9 percent of all government revenue); state personal income taxes (8 percent of all government revenue) which are generally even less progressive, in fact far less progressive, than their federal counterpart; and state corporate income taxes (1.8 percent of all government revenue). Meanwhile, more than 43 percent of federal taxes and 65 percent of state and local taxes are mildly to extremely *regressive*: federal excise and customs taxes, contributions for social insurance at both the federal and state level, property taxes, and, most regressive of all, sales taxes. Together these taxes account for more than 41 percent of federal revenue, 65 percent of state and local revenue, and together just over 50 percent of all government revenue.[2] This is scandalous. It defies any reasonable standard of justice to impose higher rates of taxation upon the poor than upon the rich. There is likewise a high degree of regressivity in our state and local taxes. The effective tax rates for America's state and local taxes are roughly 12.5 percent for the poorest one-fifth, 9.5 percent for the middle fifth, under 7 percent for the richest fifth, and less than 6 percent for the richest 1 percent (less than half the rate paid by the poor).[3] Conservatives who advocate a flat tax for America already have what they profess to want: effective overall tax rates for the rich that are no higher than what they are for the poor. In this context, making the federal income tax a flat tax would be to create a decidedly regressive overall tax structure wherein more revenue is to be raised from regressive taxes than from progressive ones. However, since America's regressive taxes are more regressive than our progressive taxes are progressive, we are already living in a reverse Robin Hood world where, overall, we tax the middle and lower classes at rates higher than those imposed on the rich.

A third oddity and defect with the American tax structure is its bottom heaviness; in other words, we have a relatively and unusually high proportion of taxes raised by sub-national (state and local) governments. Over the past fifty years or so, state and local taxation as a percentage of gross domestic products has risen by more than a third, from 6.8 percent of GDP to more than 9.3 percent of GDP. This represents an increase from 28 percent of all taxes levied in America to 35 percent of all taxes.[4] It stands in sharp contrast to most European countries where nearly all taxes are levied by the national government and the rate structure is heavily progressive. The most recent big jump in the bottom heaviness of America's tax structure occurred in the 1980s when President Reagan sought tax cuts for the wealthy and dramatic increases in military expenditures. A Democratic Congress went along with both but insisted upon keeping social welfare expenditures largely intact. The consequences of the bargain were an explosion in the size of the national debt (in recent decades, it has been Republican presidents, not Democratic ones, who have presided over massive debt growth) *and* a sharp reduction in grants-in-aid to states and localities.

As the federal government "solved" its budget crisis by passing along the costs to future generations and to sub-national governments, the states immediately felt a budget crisis of their own—one caused by the loss of so much federal aid. Their ultimate "solution" was to raise state taxes and to reduce state aid to localities. In turn, this created a budget crisis at the local level. The localities had no one lower to pass the bill to—no one, that is, except local taxpayers. Over the past few decades, therefore, we have seen a marked rise in the kinds of taxes localities generally rely upon (sales taxes, school property taxes, and town/city property taxes), at exactly the time when the far more progressive federal income tax has been lowered, especially for the wealthiest.

Aside from the reverse Robin Hood effects entailed, another concern is how far American tax policy has deviated from conventional wisdom about how to best tax and spend. Nearly 500 years ago, Niccolò Machiavelli may have been among the first to caution leaders that government is wise to do the things people find unpleasant, like tax them, quickly and all at once (to get it over with and to prevent people from dwelling on the unpleasant); conversely, Machiavelli also argues that leaders ought to spend money on programs for the people (to do pleasant things) slowly and gradually, so that they might enjoy it. From the Reagan era forward, we have created an unwise policy of imposing "large ticket item" taxes at least three different times a year: April 15 when income taxes are due, September when school taxes are due, and January when town/city taxes are due. This drawn out schedule of tax payment is a good way to incite discontent and unrest, especially in a country of "what's in it for me?" "individualists" who have been encouraged by capitalism to ignore the public good and to be suspicious of public approaches to our common problems. Only a far more civic-minded or generous population is likely to have little or no resentment for having large tax bills imposed upon them several times a year.

While American governments raise money in ways that are unwise and unfair, they spend money in ways that are equally undesirable. First of all, we spend far too much of our governmental revenue subsidizing the rich, especially considering how obscenely rich our wealthy are. In the previous chapter, we already saw that corporate welfare (for example, special tax breaks and subsidies available only to large businesses) is far more generous than "conventional" welfare (for the poor). Housing subsidies are the other enormous boondoggle of aid to the rich. In fact, measured in dollars, the single biggest government program is the tax deduction for interest paid on home mortgages. A "tax expenditure," money "spent" in the form of never collecting it in the first place (because a special tax deduction is conferred), this policy entails a housing subsidy of enormous proportions, one which benefits the rich far more than the middle class and benefits the poorest (who cannot afford home ownership) not at all. Direct government subsidies of housing for the poor amount to a pittance in comparison. In fact, the value of mortgage interest deductions just for those with annual incomes above $100,000 exceeds the Housing and Urban Development department's entire budget. A housing policy that spends far more on the rich than the poor is particularly deplorable in light of all the other disadvantages faced by the poor such as red zoning by banks, which makes it difficult to get mortgages in poorer or non-white neighborhoods and imposes higher rates if those obstacles are overcome; the relative lack of economic opportunity; geographic immobility which tends to accompany economic immobility; and the artificially high cost of homes in minority communities. No, the distribution of costs in general, beyond purely housing costs, is not kind to America's poor. Stores in poor and/or minority neighborhoods charge far more than those found in more affluent communities. Consumer information, always difficult to attain, is especially elusive from the poor. Economies of scale are likewise more elusive insofar as it is difficult to stock up on well-priced items when there is mounting debt rather than surplus in a family budget.

Spending so much time, money, and effort feeding the avarice of our privileged, perhaps it is not surprising that so little is done to subsidize our poor. Poverty relief programs are notoriously bad here. The effect of America's taxes and poverty relief transfer programs reduces overall poverty by just 28.5 percent. In contrast, European countries collectively have tax and poverty relief transfers that reduce overall poverty by more than 60 percent. The effect on child poverty per se is especially anemic. U.S. tax transfer policy reduces child poverty by barely 13 percent. European countries reduce it by roughly 40 percent.[5] Maybe this is no surprise. As a percentage of gross domestic product, the United States spends little more than 2 percent on social welfare. Social welfare spending in America was dramatically *reduced* in 1996 when Aid to Families with Dependent Children (AFDC), the nation's primary welfare program, was phased out in favor of a new, stingier, and more restrictive program, Temporary Assistance to Needy Families (TANF), which imposed both significantly lower payments to the poor and introduced time limits on how long one can receive benefits regardless of ongoing need. By contrast, Denmark, Finland, Norway, and Sweden collectively on average spend nearly 14 percent of their GDP (roughly seven times the relative rate of welfare expenditure in the United States) on social welfare programs. No wonder child poverty in America stands at nearly 23 percent of children in contrast to the 6-percent rate in the aforementioned countries.[6] Who could have guessed that poverty might bear some relationship to policies that overtax the poor and overspend on the rich?

Of course, poverty in America also has a lot to do with classism and racism. Hatred of the poor and hatred of those groups, non-white, that constitute disproportionately large segments of the poor, lies at the very heart of American "culture." It resides hidden (but not very well hidden) in our core mythology: the American dream. If *anyone* can make it in America, if all it takes is any combination of hard work, talent, and luck, if, over time, enough talent or enough hard work tends to prevail over even surprising amounts of bad luck, what does that say about those who don't make it in America, those who remain mired in poverty throughout a lifetime or, worse still, across many generations? Obviously, *they* must be *dumb and lazy*. Perhaps they are unlucky too, but since luck eventually turns, only their inferiority can explain their inferior position. In this way, disdain for the poor and for minorities is *embedded in* the American dream. It is only by unveiling the American dream as a hoax and a lie—only by unveiling the biases of capitalism, which really reward privilege and money far more than talent or industry, and the biases of pluralism and constitutionalism, which create gridlock to lock in policies that favor the rich and harm the poor—that we can begin to escape our education in blaming victims.

THE NEW TRIBALISM: LOCALISM AND FEDERALISM

Many countries have severe problems with tribalism. The word "tribe" has a primitive connotation and it may be racist to the extent that it is more likely to be used to describe non-white ethnicities than white ones. A better or more precise word for "tribe" may be "nation," which despite its frequent misuse as perfectly synonymous with "country" literally means a people or ethnicity: a population with a common identity, history, language, and set of customs. In many countries, loyalty to ethnic groups significantly trumps and undermines loyalty to the country at large. In the United States today, loyalties to ethnic groups are relatively muted and are in most cases compromised by significant levels of intermingling and intermarriage. However, there *are* considerable loyalties, allegiances, and alliances to one's locality and state and they serve to significantly undermine the likelihood of pursuing country-wide approaches to problems that seem to require them. Maybe such local and state ties can be called America's tribalism or a new tribalism. There is, after all, something unnecessarily divisive and counterproductive about allegiances that undermine our common identity and that render significantly unlikely the kinds of policy solutions Americans desperately need.

The institutional basis for this new tribalism is federalism, the division of power between *levels* of government. With federalism, power is divided between the states on the one hand and the federal government on the other; it is also divided *among* the states insofar as they compete not only with the federal government but with one another as well. In a sense, federalism is just an extension of pluralism—yet another means of dispersing power, this one a dispersal of power between and among levels of government. Like the larger pluralism, federalism is a great way to prevent government from having enough power to do great harm but it is an even better way to prevent government from having enough power to do much good. And maybe that's the whole point; federalism helps protect the rich from having to pay more taxes, it protects suburbanites from having to pay for helping to fix our generally neglected cities, it protects whites from racial integration and in a myriad of other ways, and it facilitates the abdication of social and collective responsibilities.

Local governments are not even mentioned in the U.S. Constitution. Formally speaking, they are merely aspects of state government power, chartered into being or removed from existence at the whim of their states.

However, in the context of the hyper-dispersal of power that is American politics, localities come to enjoy genuine autonomy and intensively compete with one another and the states and federal government as well. In many areas of the country, local loyalties exceed statewide ones. A prime example is Connecticut, often described as more like a series of fiefdoms than a unified state. Here, local taxes exceed state taxes, enormous disparities between rich and poor towns and cities go relatively unmodified by the state, and class and race based segregation is simply enormous. Even the phone books are divided into section by town such that it is impossible to look up someone without knowing where she or he resides.

Ultimately, the trouble with localism and federalism is that they generally make efforts to hold accountable corporations and the rich impossible. If a state or locality wishes to impose higher taxes on corporations, corporations have only to threaten to move to another locality or state to dismantle the initiative. If a state or locality wishes to impose more regulation to minimize pollution or maximize workers' rights, the same threat to leave is effective in thwarting change. This works as well in the opposite direction: large businesses can extort concessions by threatening to relocate. For example, large businesses can demand tax breaks by threatening to move to another state or country if they don't get them. Sports franchises have nearly turned this into a science, threatening to move to another city if their city doesn't pay for most or all of a new stadium and sometimes announcing a deal with a new city only to bring the offer back to their current city as leverage for a larger subsidy.

The initiative for trying to get corporations to relocate may instead come entirely from interstate or intercity competition. Virginia, for example, has advertised that they are a "right to work" state where legal obstacles to unionization are so intense, corporations are guaranteed a non-unionized—in other words, low paid—work force. Louisiana, with its "chemical alley" and horrific environmental record, has made it clear that most any corporation may legally dump most anything most anywhere.

Even some apologists for capitalism are among those calling for more powerful national government and less state autonomy as a means of cleaning up obviously excessive abuse and corruption in American businesses. For example, John C. Bogle, founder and former CEO of the Vanguard mutual fund, convincingly argues that the American investment system often destroys more value than it creates, insofar as it has become a "manager's capitalism" instead of an "owner's capitalism," a "rent-a-stock" system instead of an "own-a-stock" system, a system of mergers instead of a system of production, and a "salesmanship" system instead of a "stewardship" system. This new and unpleasant version of American capitalism rewards corrupt and greedy business elites and managers and harms owners and investors. Bogle's proposed solution is to "preempt the

multiple state laws" under which American corporations have been chartered since the country's founding, and perhaps to create *federal* rather
than state charters for fiduciary institutions and maybe even for business
corporations.[7] He may be far too optimistic about the good old days
when capitalism was not as crass (but perhaps only because it was even
more elitist then) *and* about capitalists' potential to pursue unmitigated
greed in some areas (for the corporation) but not others (for themselves).
Still, Bogle makes a good point about state autonomy and state discretion
over business matters serving as a facilitator of more corporate corruption
and more economic inefficiency.

Quite apart from *promoting* corporate corruption, corporate welfare, tax
evasion, unfair and anti-labor business practices, and pollution, the trouble
with localism and federalism is that it undermines our *national* identity. If
we cannot be Americans in our common concern for economic efficiency,
fair taxes, labor rights, a clean environment, and other social issues, then
what does hold us together as Americans? Greed? That just seems to tear us
further and further apart. Our foreign policy? As we will see in the next
chapter, this is, for the most part, a history of raping and pillaging most of
the rest of the world rather than one another. It is *not* an identity for which
Americans can be unified and proud. What is desperately needed in America and what is very much undermined by our "new tribalism" is a common
national identity that has something to do with viable visions of democracy
and justice, not still more competition, greed, and corruption.

POLITICAL CULTURE: FALSE IMAGE OF OURSELVES

We Americans have a remarkably high opinion of ourselves. In overwhelming numbers, we believe the things we have been told about ourselves,
things we have told ourselves and each other, since our grade school days.
Specifically, most all of us believe that we live in a democracy, that we will
typically go to great lengths to defend other democracies, and that we will
often risk our own well-being to help create democracies where none have
previously existed. Relatedly, we believe that we are among the world's foremost advocates of human rights that are most likely to be abrogated by the
governments in the world least like our own. We believe that we are the
world's most generous people, generous almost to a fault, perhaps actually
generous to a fault—always giving away unprecedented sums to our own
poor and especially to the world's needy, stepping in to save the day whenever crisis (storm, famine, or war) strikes or simply to alleviate ongoing
poverty in the neediest of nations. Yes, we are a caring people we tell ourselves; we are paying attention to where we are needed and ready and able
to help at a moment's notice.

We tell ourselves, further, that one of the best things about our democracy is that we have created an open society, where all points of view are allowed and where there is no place for the banality of political censorship. Our openness enriches our diversity. We tolerate diverse perspectives just as we tolerate diverse peoples. Moreover, we say that we celebrate our diversity. Our Statue of Liberty acts as a welcome beacon to all in the world who wish to come here for our unparalleled freedoms and our unparalleled economic opportunities: Come! Join us! We say that our society is enriched by the seas of new peoples we have welcomed here and will continue to welcome here. We say that we are a melting pot society where diverse peoples arrive, intermingle, even intermarry, and enrich one another and our fabulous society. We say that we are a land of unique individuals—fiercely independent and free-minded, deep and special, even if at times a bit rough and tumble. What a wonderful self-image we have! The trouble is, it's almost entirely *untrue*.

Democracy? We have a government that is *structured*, in its pluralism and constitutionalism, to *resist* the will of the majority. Largely because of this, more than half of us don't even bother to vote in Presidential elections and more than three-quarters of us don't vote in other election years. Defenders of other democracies? Selfless creators of new democracies? As we will see in the next chapter, the democracies of the world have generally known no greater enemy than the United States of America, and when our government has put itself in the position to impose governments on other peoples, we have created far, far more fascist regimes than democratic ones.

Champions of human rights? Is this something we can even claim with a straight face? It is, after all, our *formal* policies that authorize the use of "low" intensity torture, transfer of detainees to many of our dictatorial allies for high intensity torture (to be carried out as per our directions and in consultation with our government officials), and targeted assassinations. Victims of all three of these types of abuse are more likely than not to be *incorrectly* identified as "undesirable" persons. Abu Ghraib and Guantanamo[8] were not aberrations to be corrected; they are policies being maintained. The United States has also refused to join the International Criminal Court designed to prevent and prosecute the worst of human rights violations. We are among just a few significant countries to withhold membership and support and we are the primary obstacle to the court's effectiveness.

Generous? We have already seen that our social welfare spending is scandalously low and falls very far short of the norms set by comparable countries. Our record of foreign assistance is even worse. Roughly half of our foreign aid is military aid, not humanitarian aid, and half of all our aid goes to just two key allies: Israel and Egypt.[9] Giving little more than two tenths of 1 percent of our gross national income (GNI) in humanitarian assistance, we rank pathetically toward the very bottom of western countries in humanitarian foreign aid as a percentage of GNI and we occasionally even rank near or in second (with or behind Saudi Arabia) in absolute dollars contributed.[10] Many countries with far, far less give relatively much more. We are also *opponents*, not *proponents*, of the Millennium Development Goals movement, which calls upon all countries to give development aid amounting to at least seven-tenths of 1 percent of their GDP. That would force us to increase our foreign aid more than three-fold.

Caring? Americans are all too often uninformed, misinformed, and apathetic about politics, especially politics elsewhere in the world. We know scandalously little about the world's geography, history, governments, peoples, and needs. Maybe ignorance is the privilege of the privileged. Maybe it is a psychological defense that fends off ownership of our role in causing so many of the world's woes. In any event, as we will see in the next chapter, when most crises hit most of the world's peoples, there can be little hope or expectation that Americans will take much notice, let alone help.

An open society tolerating, if not encouraging, all points of view? No. We Americans tolerate everything from liberal Democrats to conservative Republicans but we don't do well outside those very limited parameters. We have already seen that our speech rights have not worked very well for our anarchists, communists, and socialists.[11] But maybe what is most surprising is that for all of our abstract celebration of our openness and freedom, we are very quick to want to silence those who offer radically different views and fundamental critiques of our government or society. For example, when Venezuelan President Hugo Chavez went to the United Nations and called President Bush the devil and when Iranian President Mahmoud Ahmadinejad went there to defend Islamism and Iran's autonomy in deciding if and when to build nuclear weapons, huge majorities of Americans, unhappy to see foreigners criticize our government and our leaders, were horrified that they were allowed to speak at American universities. Slightly smaller majorities were horrified that they were allowed to speak at the U.N., apparently not terribly aware that the U.N. does not fall within U.S. territory or jurisdiction.

Welcoming diversity? Despite all the hoopla about them, Ellis Island and the Statue of Liberty are really, truthfully, monuments to very ugly chapters in American history. Throughout most of its existence, Ellis Island imposed strict and eugenicist limits on immigration, quotas that especially limited immigration from Eastern Europe, Asia, and Africa because their populations were considered inferior to Western Europe's. When the country faced acute labor shortages in the late nineteenth and early twentieth centuries, spates of mostly western Europeans were allowed entry. Around this history, we have built a great mythology exaggerating the destitution with which immigrants arrived, the welcome they received, the opportunities they were granted, and the successes they enjoyed. While many of these immigrants often arrived relatively penniless or had their money stolen by corrupt American officials upon arrival, the fact that they could afford passage meant that they were *not* among Europe's poorest. More importantly, they were generally affluent enough to arrive literate (at least in a European language) and with a skill or trade. Their experiences upon arrival were typically not stories of pleasant welcome and rapid success. Government officials asked many potential new immigrants if they were anarchists. Those who said "no" were sent back to Europe along with those who said "yes." The only acceptable answer was "What's an anarchist?" Those who even knew what the word meant were deemed potentially dangerous. Strange reasoning was at work here but perhaps it helped assure that newer Americans would fit in with older ones (and current ones) who likewise knew (and know) too little about politics. If they made it past Ellis Island, they faced enormous ethnic biases. Their stories are filled as much with fear and heartache as eventual modest success. Many of those who could eventually afford return passage elected to go back to their country of origin, choosing it as a lesser of two evils.

Ellis Island was also the site of the forced deportation of political dissidents like Alexander Berkman, Emma Goldman, and others. And when Holocaust concentration camp survivors sought desperately to find refuge in the United States, as they sat days in New York harbor awaiting a decision, they must have thought what better example than themselves of huddled masses yearning to be free. But because they were Jews, undesirable to most Americans, they were sent back to Europe, back to the overflowing Cypriot refugee camps, and eventually even back to the former death camps converted into refugee centers. The America that celebrates itself as welcoming those seeking freedom instead preferred sending Holocaust victims back to the places of their torture and the sites of their families' mass murder rather than offering any refuge, let alone welcome. Of course many decades later, with our now relatively *low* rates of economic mobility, it is hard to imagine why we would be anyone's first choice for escape from crushing poverty or persecution.

Melting pot? The optimistic types who believe the melting pot myth sometimes quibble about the analogy. Do diverse peoples really meld together? Are we more like a salad bowl or a bouillabaisse? Do the different "ingredients," in this case nationalities, all get thrown in together but retain their unique character and flavor? But is this really America? The eugenicist quotas of the nineteenth century and first half of the twentieth century meant that many "flavors" were never included in significant amounts. Since then, we've gotten rid of the embarrassingly racist quotas but have created in their stead a system in which the numbers of immigrants allowed are even more restricted and preference is given to those with relatives already here.

The implication is that the racial biases remain: we won't let in as many non-white people now because non-whites are less likely to have relatives already here given our racist quotas back then. The sad truth is that *illegal* immigration has created more diversity than legal immigration. Perhaps it is just as well that so many Chicanas and Chicanos have ignored our warnings about (re?)entering the parts of the United States we stole from Mexico. As a result, America does have more diversity than we welcomed, despite our best efforts to stop it. Even so, the resulting "pot" is more assimilation pot than melting pot, for to make it in America, one generally must behave white and middle class (or higher). Certainly, we can eat our ethnic foods, we can celebrate what holidays we like, and we can wear "traditional" clothing, but if we reject "standard" (read: white) English or the basic parameters of a consumer-oriented and materialist lifestyle, we will be considered seriously weird and find ourselves less than welcome. Multicultural consumerism, a mere variation of existing practice, is not a perceived threat to the existing order; anti-consumerism and multi-lingualism, direct challenges to current practices, are.

Tolerant? What do we make of our unrelenting racism? Overt expressions of racist hatred remain frighteningly widespread, as suggested by the recent nationwide spate of dozens of lynch nooses left in places frequented by African Americans. Openly racist organizations retain strong memberships and remain active across the country: the Ku Klux Klan (with its highest percentage of the population as members in Indiana, not Mississippi), neo-Nazi groups (even stronger in the rust belt than the Deep South), and skin head groups (most active in the Pacific Northwest). But, by far, our biggest problem is the racism of ordinary Americans who claim not to be racist at all and yet oppose most everything many African Americans could use for opportunity and success. Solid majorities of white Americans oppose Affirmative Action and call it reverse discrimination but voice no opposition to special privileges that principally benefit whites, such as legacy admissions to college. They criticize colleges and universities that slightly reduce grade point average and board score requirements for *minority* students in order to attain needed racial diversity but they approve of the same measures for *white* applicants who can help fill out the marching band or the soccer team. They oppose social welfare for the poor but make no complaints about corporate welfare. They oppose housing subsidies for the poor but staunchly defend them for themselves (the mortgage interest deduction). They complain bitterly about "black nationalist" leaders like Al Sharpton, Louis Farrakhan, or even Jesse Jackson, who seek to mobilize African American voters, but voice no complaints about felon exclusion laws that exist to minimize black suffrage rights. They profess no obviously racist sentiments but would worry about having to sell their homes (to protect their equity of course) if African Americans were to move into their neighborhood. They claim education is most important but oppose spending more on poor urban school districts and even more vociferously oppose busing and racial integration of schools. This is America's biggest and most powerful racism: the racism of the self-proclaimed "non-racists."

Rugged individualism? On the basis of what? It certainly can't be because some of us are avidly materialist consumers preferring one kind of product and others of us are the same preferring a different line of products. Is it because our founding fathers were revolutionaries? No. For revolutionaries, they were remarkably conservative. They led a taxpayer revolt that did not challenge the pre-existing social order but merely took over its reigns and profits. Is it because we live in a hyper-competitive capitalist economy? No, America features many more sheepish consumers than wolfish profiteers. Is it because our forbearers had to settle and tame a new continent, confronting and overcoming the risks of empty land, isolation, and privation? No, the land they "tamed" were already occupied. They needed to evict its occupants and owners and did so with a genocide against Native Americans. Afterward, much of the hardest labor entailed in working the land was done by enslaved Africans, who provided whites not only with unpaid labor but also with a false sense of superiority.[12] Rival European imperialists, French and Russian, were made to believe that they weren't strong enough to defend their possessions and were intimidated into selling them. Half of Mexico was invaded and taken. Military conquest, genocide, enslavement, intimidation, resettlement of others' lands—there was nothing new, unique, or individuating about these actions. They constituted the very nature of the bulk of the previous history of the whole world.

What may be most telling is the frequency with which outside observers of America and of Americans have concluded that Americans are overwhelmingly and surprisingly alike. By far the most famous of these observers was Alexis de Tocqueville who, in his classic *Democracy in America* (1835 and 1840), was perhaps the first to note the disturbing sameness of Americans. In his most famous passage, he claimed there was no other country "in which there is so little independence of mind and real freedom of discussion as in America."[13] He referred to this sameness of thought and speech as both a leveling of opinion and a tyranny of the majority and, while it had some positive effects (providing some measure of social cohesiveness in a pluralist polity), it was, for the most part, a worrisome thing. It was potentially a source of abuse of the very few who did not conform adequately (hence a *tyranny* of the majority) and perhaps, worst of all, it was indicative of a significant lack of intellectual rigor. A vibrant society of critical thinkers is very unlikely to come to the same conclusions and share the same prejudices.

Much more recently, another famous Frenchman, Jean Baudrillard, also noted with alarm an extreme sameness and mindlessness among Americans in this strange land where bank lobbies look like churches and where Disneyland is considered real. In his 1986 *America*, he observed that there is a pleasant, if vacuous, gentleness that pervades Americans. According to Baudrillard's observations, we Americans insist on mindless laughter, unrelenting laughter—laughter commanded by laugh tracks such that it is the television screen itself that is laughing and having a good time and it is only the disobedient who are left alone in consternation.[14] For Americans, intelligence "is merely a particular cast of mind in which one should not indulge unduly."[15] America's "easy life knows no pity. Its logic is a pitiless one. If utopia has already been achieved, then unhappiness does not exist, the poor are no longer credible" and there can be no real memory of the past. The Native-American genocide did not happen, slavery did not happen, Vietnam did not happen, and so on.[16] In short, Baudrillard has written what perhaps most everyone *except* Americans seem to know: that we Americans have a false image of ourselves, that we are masters of self-delusion, and our delusions are, for the most part, delusions of grandeur.

When confronted with such disillusionment, it is tempting to retreat into denial. Baudrillard can be dismissed as anti-American and *this* book can be dismissed as the work of a self-hating American. However, nothing could be further from the truth. America is *not* our inept government. *Nor* is it our pathological economy. America is nothing more or less than we Americans ourselves and it is out of a love for America so defined that this book is written. Furthermore, to read Baudrillard's *America* is to see that he has more than a fair measure of affection for us. The critical point here, however, is that our inept pluralist and constitutionalist government and our corrupt and abusive capitalism do us great harm both individually and collectively and that, if we do not abandon our self-delusions, we will be in no position to realize how badly we need fundamental changes in our political and economic order. Indeed, there may be little wrong with America that couldn't be fixed, or at least dramatically improved, with a more democratic, majoritarian, and socialist political society.

Even with our deeply rooted political and economic problems, when crisis strikes others both here and abroad, most of us have, as our first impulse anyway, the desire to help. The trouble sets in afterward. Too many of us stop and do little or nothing because we remember that our own economic position is precarious (thanks to capitalism) and that our government (thanks to pluralism) is not likely to do much to help *us* if and when we need it. No, it is better to pinch our pennies and save for a rainy day.

Because our government isn't all it should be, we don't behave as gener-
ously as we would like to be able to. When we get the impulse to help the
poor overseas, again we stop, partly for the same reasons but also because
too many of us are misinformed and falsely think that our government is
already giving them huge sums. When it comes time to elect officials to
make policies about domestic and foreign aid, uninformed, misinformed,
and correct only in a vague awareness that, for some reason, nothing ever
changes here anyway, half of us choose not to vote at all. A majority among
the other half, again often out of insecurity and misinformation, rushes to
vote for candidates who appeal to voters' narrow sense of *self*-interest and
who pledge to *reduce* social welfare and foreign humanitarian assistance.

In America, there is no shortage of well-intentioned people. We have no
shortage of the devout, the pious, the kind-hearted, or the empathetic.
What we are missing is a mechanism of good government and equitable
economics that allows good intention to convert into action rather than
stymie it. Maybe Adam Smith and James Madison had it exactly backward:
in capitalist and pluralist America, out of private virtue (a natural inclina-
tion to help) comes public vice (*in*action). In any event, even to begin to
overcome the structural flaws in our political system and our self-delusions
defending these flaws, we will likely need something else in short supply
here: leadership.

LEADERSHIP, AMERICAN STYLE

In America, we generally aspire to have a political system that features both
leadership and representation—perhaps not realizing that these two goals
are not immediately compatible. The goal of representation seems to imply
that the public possesses a reasonably good idea of what they want and the
political order should be structured in such a way that governing officials
are expected to, perhaps even required to, try to provide the public with a
reasonably good approximation of that which they want. The concept of
representative government, at a minimum, implies that government officials should be held accountable by the public and certainly subject to at
least eventual removal from office if they deviate too far from the public's
desires.

Leadership, on the other hand, seems to imply the presence of public figures who think and advocate something more or different (and hopefully
better) than the public. These leading figures must somehow be able to persuade, cajole, or maybe even coerce the public into going along with or even
endorsing an idea that originated with a leader rather than themselves.
There are some who believe that coercion cannot be genuine leadership,
that true leadership requires a dialogue of some sort between leader and

follower, a dialogue that is essentially persuasion and not coercion.[17] Such a position may be counter-intuitive insofar as it seems to imply that successful dictators such as Hitler and Stalin were *not* leaders. The political systems they directed may have been nightmares but it seems that they were horrific precisely to the extent that they were successful in leading so many others to take abusive action. More to the point, this view of leadership as incompatible with coercion may underestimate the extent to which coercion *is* persuasive and the extent to which coercive regimes sustain enthusiastic support from powerful minorities or even majorities. Put another way, the persuasion of some is what makes possible the coercion of others and the worst of tyrants are powerful as much or more because of the appearance of power as the reality of it. In more democratic systems, followers may influence leaders more openly and safely in various ways ranging from petitioning to protesting. However, in any kind of political environment, a leader is someone who is more successful in directing others than in being directed by them.

For representation and leadership to be compatible, we must imagine a leader persuading a relatively empowered public in such a way that they come to think differently about an issue or issues. The people must then be able to meaningfully consent to and endorse the new idea, making it their own will and, in so doing, making implementation of the idea a matter of representation insofar as it is what the public *now* wants even though its ultimate origin comes from the leader and not the public. Is this what happens in America? Do we get both leadership and representation? One but not the other? Sadly, what typically happens here is that we get precious little of either.

In general, America's politicians don't seem to possess any of the key characteristics of leaders: vision, facility in engaging in persuasive dialogue with followers, and power to create change. Given all they say and do, America's politicians certainly don't seem like visionaries. The occasional visionary we may find here—for example, perhaps, Martin Luther King—is quite noticeably *not* a politician. The rare politician who genuinely seems interested in achieving meaningful change and who tries to escape the binds of partisanship and, most especially, pluralism is thoroughly frustrated and stymied and apt to leave office early. Perhaps the best example here is former Republican Senator Warren Rudman of New Hampshire who left office after two terms, complaining that there was simply no way to get anything significant accomplished within the U.S. Senate or within American politics generally for that matter. Most likely, prospective politicians bent on meaningful change learn early on, well before establishing enough success to reach high office, that American politics is not a place where meaningful change can be initiated. As a result, they are less apt to stay in politics than those who are servicing their egos and ambitions more than the public well-being. Moreover, those who make it to the highest offices in American politics are quite frequently second or third generation politicians, making it easy to wonder if we have an elective aristocracy instead of a democracy.

It is quite telling that America's politicians hardly engage in any meaningful dialogue with constituents. Instead, almost all of the communication from our politicians has to do with getting them elected, and getting elected in America has precious little to do with meaningful conversation with people. The reality of our electoral process is that roughly one-third of our voters will lean heavily and immediately toward the Democrat, one-third will lean heavily and immediately toward the Republican, and the real contest will be over who can win the one-third that could break either way. If the race is at all close, the one-third who start out undecided will itself break into thirds: one-third that break toward the Democrat, one-third that break toward the Republican, and one-third who remain undecided, sometimes until the last possible moment. The election will hinge on this last group: the one-third of the one-third—our most uncertain voters. Because this group of voters is by far the least knowledgeable and least informed, a successful political campaign will be one that strikes pleasant sounding general themes such as "proven leadership" or "it's time for a change"—things that mean almost nothing but sound appealing. Under these circumstances, the *typical* circumstances in American politics, engaging in a meaningful dialogue with voters, taking clear positions on issues, and trying to persuade voters to support a candidate for such clear positions is a formula for defeat.

Even when our politicians pretend that they want to hear what their constituents desire, they are almost always looking for votes and support rather than genuinely listening or communicating in a substantive way. Questionnaires sent home to constituents are an amusing if somewhat disheartening case in point. A careful look at the questions themselves reveal that they are designed to manipulate the constituents rather than to allow a flow of information that might persuade the politician or simply inform her or him of how the constituents feel. Maybe more than anything else, they are designed to provide false data that will enable the politician to say that she or he *is* doing what constituents desire. Consider, for example, the question I once received from a former Congressman of mine, a question not unlike others from politicians, except, perhaps, in how obvious it was in its design to generate such false data. The question sent home to all his constituents read something like this:

> Given the accident free record of the use of nuclear power in the U.S. Navy, should the United States explore the expansion of nuclear energy instead of becoming even more dangerously dependent upon foreign countries to meet our energy needs?

Well, first I laughed. Then I wondered what happened in other branches of the military and in civilian use that kept my Congressman from mentioning an accident free use of nuclear energy in places other than the navy. But, most of all, I realized that this was certainly not part of a sincere effort to learn what his constituents thought. Instead, like almost all of our politicians before and since, every time I heard from this man, he was trying to get me to vote for him and/or trying to misrepresent what I thought. His questionnaires were designed to collect data to suggest that the way he had already decided he was going to vote in the House conformed to the wishes of his constituents and perhaps to sway the grossly uninformed to think the way he did. They were not designed to accurately measure what his constituents thought. I can't think of a single time he promoted genuine dialogue about policy or tried to persuade me (unless one wants to consider the insipid questionnaires acts of persuasion).

Even in politicians' construction of vague campaign themes designed to influence undecided voters and win elections, the process reveals that anything but leadership is occurring. Political campaigns do *not* sit down to evaluate what their candidate really wants to do and how best to describe that in a vague theme that might best appeal to the electorate. Rather, they sit with public opinion surveys about what the electorate already thinks at the moment and try to figure out how best to cash in on that with a vague theme that is likely to be popular but need not have any real connection to their candidate. It was in this manner that George Herbert Walker Bush became the candidate seeking to become "the education President." The directionality involved here is all wrong for it to involve leadership. A true leader would have a vision of something new and better and would proceed to sell that vision along with herself or himself. In America, our politicians start with what the public already thinks, wrap themselves in that, and hope to do whatever they want, even if totally unrelated, after winning or returning to office.

Could this be a kind of dishonest leadership but leadership nonetheless? Not really. In the United States, our politicians will never have the power to escape the stagnating confines of pluralism. If they are lying and cheating in hopes of doing some good after hoodwinking the voters, they are apt to find that they will never possess the power to achieve ends that might justify the means.

If we fail at leadership, do we at least have reasonably good representation? Again, the answer seems to be no. How can representation be functional in a country where half don't vote even in Presidential election years and three quarters don't vote in other election years? Some would say that non-voters offer their tacit consent. However, this does not fit with what we know about non-voters. They are hardly a contented lot. As a group, they are poorer and less educated than voters.[18] Their apparent belief that American

politics doesn't help neglected people like themselves can as easily be characterized as savvy insight as apathy. Either way, it is clearly not consent.

Furthermore, for representation to be functional, politicians would have
to both possess and correctly identify their policy preferences, voters would
need to be well aware of them, and, after election, politicians would have
to generally keep the promises they made to get elected. None of that happens much in America. Our politicians typically hide policy preferences,
avoiding controversial issues and speaking in vague generalities and nearly
vacuous campaign themes. Only about one-third of our voters even consider the *stated* policy positions of candidates. Far fewer seek the *real* policy
inclinations of candidates so often hidden behind misleading rhetoric or
even outright lies. But it is this final requirement of representation, the ability to keep and implement campaign promises, that is palpably absent in
the United States and it is this absence that crushes all possibility of adequate representation in America. It is probably the case that most of our
politicians are fairly well-intentioned people who strive to work for what
they honestly believe to be in the best interests of the people. They may play
many Machiavellian power games along the way—conspire, deceive, or
even lie and cheat—but their hope may be that what is good for their political career will empower them to work for a better America. The trouble
is, and it is a positively damning trouble, the nature of pluralism is such
that our politicians will always be thwarted in their policy preferences and
little if anything will be accomplished. Politicians cannot deliver their
promises because the pluralist distribution of power doesn't afford them
any significant power with which to do so. Voters cannot force politicians
to deliver a better America because they have no more power than the
politicians. Even if they became inclined to always vote *against* incumbents
(and in the absence of political knowledge and sophistication they have a
strongly opposite, pro-incumbent bias), all that could change is the specific
people occupying the political positions that offer insufficient power to
change things significantly.

Our peculiar election system only aggravates our lack of genuine representation. Our system of first-past-the-post plurality elections with single
member districts (wherein we elect just one person, whoever gets the most
votes, to represent each district) guarantees the presence of a two party system. This, along with our uni-ideological society, and our non-responsible
party system, means that we are typically choosing among two candidates
who are, in most regards, largely the same. We would be far better served
and far more democratic if we had proportional representation, a multi-
party system, multiple member districts, and responsible political parties.
Proportional representation systems award legislative seats roughly in ac-
cordance with the percentage of seats a party wins. Its use guarantees a
multi-party system (because it gives some say to all parties that can win a

significant percentage of votes) and is generally used in conjunction with multiple member districts (that is, more than one official can come from the same district so that a party's total number of elected officials can be as numerous as the party's percentage of the votes warrants). Responsible political parties require their members to keep fairly close to the party's stated policy positions or risk expulsion from their party and a likely end to their political career. The presence of responsible parties enables voters to have a good idea of what a candidate stands for even in the absence of any information about her or him other than party affiliation. As a result, it makes policy-oriented voting as easy as America's electoral rules make it difficult.

Keeping in mind all the dysfunctions of America's election system and its place within the stagnation imposing national domestic environment of pluralism, no wonder we have had such a pathological electoral history. The nature of America's elections is such that we have witnessed very little leadership and representation but an embarrassing amount of fraud, voter ignorance, and "choices" that make most of us cringe with dismay. Many a political observer told us that the closeness of the 2000 presidential election proved that every vote matters. However, the reality proved the opposite. In fact, when only a few hundred votes separate candidates in a statewide race, it is generally impossible to get an accurate enough vote count to know who did in fact win. Instead, the winner is whoever is in a better position to steal it. Al Gore relied, unsuccessfully, on a partisan Florida Supreme Court to pursue a partial recount that, by searching for votes mostly in Democratic districts, might have stolen the election for him. George W. Bush relied, successfully, on a partisan U.S. Supreme Court to prevent any recount and thus make off with the election despite its many improprieties, including but not limited to, the misuse of felon exclusion law practices to remove minority voters from the voting rolls whenever they had the same last name as a felon in that district, obsolete and inaccurate voting machines in poorer districts and some districts' use of inappropriate and misleading ballot designs with which it was easy to mistakenly vote in an unintended way.[19] This was hardly the first dishonest American presidential election. 1960 Democratic nominee John Kennedy, who won the nomination largely due to the use of organized crime groups to steal the West Virginia primary, was helped by the Chicago Daly political machine's fabrication of votes, "winning" Illinois and thus the election against Nixon (who also was no stranger to the use of illegal campaign tactics). Even Kennedy's successor, Lyndon Johnson, was in the position of vice president only because he narrowly won his first race for the U.S. Senate seat in Texas, thanks to hundreds of people who got up from their graves moments before the polls closed and cast their ballots for him in alphabetical order. Sometimes the dead vote more reliably than the living.

The most classic example of obvious voter ignorance may be the Illinois Democratic primary of March 1986. Long-time fascist Lyndon LaRouche uprooted his unsuccessful Labor Party activities in New York to try a different tactic in Illinois. Instead of launching more minor party efforts, he attempted to gain influence within the Democratic Party. He challenged well-known gubernatorial aspirant Adlai Stevenson III for the Democratic nomination for governor. Other LaRouchees challenged mainstream Democrats for the nominations for lieutenant governor and secretary of state. At the time of voting, Illinois Democratic primary voters were caught unaware. They recognized Stevenson's name and overwhelmingly voted for him in the primary, but were uncertain of the other contests: fascist Mark Fairchild running against former State Senator and Congressman George Sangmeister in the race for lieutenant governor and fascist Janice Hart running against Aurelia Pucinski, Chicago Sanitation Board member and daughter of an influential Chicago alderman, in the race for secretary of state. Primary voters, despite being far better informed than general election voters, apparently did not recognize any of these people and, presumably on the basis of a preference for "less ethnic" names (and people), elected the two fascists. Illinois was not overrun with fascists that year and there was nothing unfair about the election. It was simply a case of uninformed voters. Given the racism central to fascism, it is perhaps ironic that ethnic biases may have played a decisive role in Fairchild's and Hart's victories. Following the primary, Stevenson, unwilling to run for office with a fascist ticket, formed another temporary party, the Real Democrats. Despite all the publicity caused by the scandalous nomination of fascists, however, many general election voters were still confused by the presence of two Democratic parties and Republicans easily swept to victory in all three races. This may be a quirky chapter in the history of American electoral politics but it proves a critical point: there can be no meaningful representation when the voters don't know much, and unfortunately, this is all too often the case among American voters.

Sometimes the results of unwise primary votes in both parties leaves general election voters with only a highly unpleasant "choice." That may have been most famously the case in the 1991 Louisiana governor's race. This culminated in a contest between the perpetually corrupt, frequently indicted and tried, and eventually convicted racketeer and extortionist, former Democratic Governor Edwin Edwards, and Neo-Nazi, former Grand Wizard of the Ku Klux Klan, Republican David Duke. Edwards won but two popular bumper stickers said it all: "Vote for the Crook. It's important," and "Better a lizard than a wizard."

When our politicians are typically obfuscators who speak in vague campaign themes drawn from polling data on the pre-existing biases of voters, even if we avoid those who engage in outright lies and frauds, it is clear that genuine leadership is not facilitated by our political processes. When our people are more likely to stay home than vote and when they frequently know little or nothing when they do vote, when the choices before them often include no desirable options and when election outcomes hinge most on the votes of those who know the least, it is clear that genuine representation is not facilitated by our political system either. Indeed, it is hard to imagine that anyone could consider this mess democratic.

THE NEW ANARCHY: THE ABDICATION OF GOVERNMENTAL RESPONSIBILITY

Republicans and now even most Democrats tell us that the era of big government, which began with Franklin Roosevelt and the New Deal and extended at least through the Lyndon Johnson administration, is over. There now appears to be a genuine consensus that government in America must be smaller, thriftier, and less ambitious, at least in all areas except war making. Liberalism has become an unpopular, if not dirty, word in the vast majority of American political constituencies. Socialism is falsely equated with communism as evil and obsolete; it has no place within the American political agenda.

What makes all this so remarkable is that, by the standards of other first world societies, America *never* had an era of big government. In an attempt to end the Great Depression and to mitigate its devastating effects—the depression being a failure of capitalism, by the way—the New Deal introduced a very modest welfare state. The heart and soul of this program were the expansion of government employment, public works projects, and a Social Security system—still a thorn in the paw of many American conservatives—which, at *that* time, provided retirement benefits starting at age 65 when the average lifespan was only 62. By the time of the Johnson administration, and largely because of its successes, the welfare state became more robust with more substantive anti-poverty provisions: a beefed up unemployment insurance program, public housing subsidies, and Aid to Families with Dependent Children. The Nixon administration, which immediately followed, began the process of paring down these programs, something that was done far more vigorously under Reagan and since. Even at their zenith in Johnson's Great Society, the rate of expenditure on social programs—what we spend on neither the military nor corporations but rather on one another for things ranging from poverty relief, to education, to healthcare, and to support for arts and culture—was far short of half of what it is in our more civilized European counterparts. We Americans have always been remarkably stingy with our government and one another. Compared to our peers, we have always paid relatively low (but regressive) taxes, been reluctant to initiate or support social programs, and have done remarkably little to use government to assure the public well-being.

Our government has always been unusually weak because it was designed primarily to avoid tyranny, not to help us solve our public problems. If our goal now is to make our government even smaller, then we are even more firmly embracing the abdication of our social and collective responsibilities. America is becoming a neo-anarchist country wherein everyone is expected to take care of themselves and no one else. Those who are not sufficiently self-supporting are simply left behind to struggle with problems, such as poverty, ill health, lack of education, lack of opportunity, crime, and the like, that really would be most effectively addressed publicly and collectively by a government and society that felt a genuine obligation to solve these problems.

A perverse form of libertarianism has been taking more and more control over the American psyche. This Americanized version of libertarianism bears little resemblance to its European counterpart wherein libertarian and anarchist impulses are wedded to socialism, and the fear of hierarchical authority calls for weakening bureaucratized hierarchies of government in order to strengthen local and socialist communities. In America, however, the new libertarian consensus emerging more and more powerfully across most of the country calls for government to stop interfering in social issues (thus, no regulation of sex lives, no bans on abortion, no bans on gay and lesbian sex, and so forth) and to keep out of economic affairs (e.g., very minimal regulation of business, low taxes, laissez-faire economics, and so on). In the final analysis, America's neo-anarchism may be a false anarchism and America's neo-libertarianism a false libertarianism. As scholar and activist Noam Chomsky has pointed out, "what's called 'libertarianism' here is unbridled capitalism. Now, that's always been opposed in the European libertarian tradition, where every anarchist has been a socialist—because the point is, if you have unbridled capitalism, you have all kinds of authority; you have *extreme* authority."[20]

America's perverse libertarianism may be reaching new levels of popularity but it rests on an American tradition that dates at least as far back as the first American flag: a snake on a yellow background with the motto *Don't tread on me* emblazoned underneath the snake. Many years later we Americans remain snake-like, for a more contemporary expression of this motto, read as outward warning to other nations *and* to other Americans cautioned to keep to themselves, would read: *Get lost. Leave me alone.* Read the other way, as a message to the reader/listener that this is not a land where others will admit of any responsibility to or for you, the motto is: *Good luck, buddy. You're on your own.* The real problem reflected in these sentiments, even beyond the social negligence they encourage, is that the very social fabric of

America is torn. A country where people want to leave others alone and be left alone is no country at all. For Americans to learn to live together and care for one another, we really need to build something distressingly new and unfamiliar: a genuine sense of sociality and community. Building that sensibility in a country where most of us have been encouraged to be politically and economically sociopathic is a tall order indeed.

There may be a bit of a Catch 22 here. As Chomsky has argued, the real source of successful activism and eventual change is not really the work of great individuals, although we may often falsely equate an individual with a given change. Instead, successful activism can only come from well-organized community with the real work being done by people who remain unknown.[21] But if it is community itself which is most under siege by the onslaughts of pluralism, capitalism, and our perverse new form of anarchism, improving things will be all the more difficult for us as Americans. To overcome our flawed government and failed society, we will need to invent more ways to build connection and trust among ourselves even before, or at least as, we try to build viable movements for change.

NOTES

1. For a precise breakdown of effective tax rates of the federal income tax and how they have changed over recent decades, see Lawrence Mishel, Jared Bernstein, and Sylvia Allegretto, *The State of Working America 2006/2007* (Ithaca, NY: ILR Press, 2007), 69, 74.

2. These calculations are made on the basis of data provided in Mishel, Bernstein, and Allegretto, *State of Working America 2006/2007* (Ithaca, NY: ILR Press, 2007), 72–73.

3. See Lawrence Mishel, Jared Bernstein and John Schmitt, *The State of Working America, 2000/2001*, 369.

4. Mishel, Bernstein, and Allegretto, *State of Working America 2006/2007*, 72.

5. Timothy M. Smeeding, "Financial Poverty in Developed Countries: The Evidence from LIS," Luxembourg Income Study Working Paper No. 155, 1997. Cited in Mishel, Bernstein, and Schmitt, *State of Working America 2000/2001*, 394.

6. Mishel, Bernstein, and Allegretto, *State of Working America 2006/2007*, 352.

7. John C. Bogle, *The Battle for the Soul of Capitalism* (New Haven: Yale University Press, 2005), 224.

8. The prisoners at Abu Ghraib prison in Iraq and at the Guantanamo naval base in the U.S. occupied portion of Cuba were rounded up largely at random. American officials hoped that they were imprisoning, at Abu Ghraib, significant numbers of Iraqi resistance fighters and, at Guantanamo, significant numbers of Al Qaeda partisans. Prisoners in both locations are being held indefinitely without charges and are being subjected to torture. Photographs of Abu Ghraib prisoner abuse brought the scandal to public light and proved especially embarrassing

because the torture involved sexual abuse (assumed to be particularly humiliating to Muslim victims). For a detailed account of the random and arbitrary nature of the incarcerations at Guantanamo and Abu Ghraib, see Seymour M. Hersh, *Chain of Command: The Road from 9/11 to Abu Ghraib* (New York: Harper-Collins, 2004).

9. This may be the price we continue to pay for the 1978 Camp David Peace Accord between Israel and Egypt and to keep these regimes safe from the overwhelming numbers of people who detest them for their various brutalities.

10. The United States ranks 20th among 22 Organization for Economic Cooperation and Development nations (western countries) in foreign aid as a percentage of gross national income. We are far short of most Scandinavian nations which give over seven-tenths of a percent of GNI to meet the international Millennium Development goal. Other western nations are well on their way toward meeting the goal. Not the United States. In 2007, we gave just over two-tenths of a percent of our GNI. Saudi Arabia occasionally ranks ahead of the U.S., even in absolute dollars, by giving over 5 percent of their gross domestic product. For details, see *Index of Global Philanthropy* (Washington, D.C.: Center for Global Prosperity, 2007), 13.

11. Fascists, too, have had their rights inappropriately curtailed but probably not as thoroughly as leftists have—perhaps because fascism is most obvious in its hyper-racism which is an extremist exaggeration of a relatively milder racist orthodoxy in America. Leftists, by contrast, are most noticeable for their anti-capitalism which represents a more direct challenge to, not exaggeration of, the American orthodoxy.

12. Famed novelist and scholar Toni Morrison has convincingly argued that white America's sense of individualism, evident in our literature, is based on the abuse of an Africanist presence. In other words, white Americans have felt like individuals (autonomous, powerful, and even solitary and/or malcontent) largely to the extent that they were not black (enslaved and mistaken for being all alike, powerless, animalistic, and savage). However, a misguided sense of superiority is not a genuine individualism. See Toni Morrison, *Playing in the Dark: Whiteness and the Literary Imagination* (New York: Vintage Books, 1993/1992), 44–51.

13. Alexis de Tocqueville, *Democracy in America*, vol. 1, ed. Phillips Bradley, (New York: Knopf, 1945/1835), 270–71.

14. Jean Baudrillard, *America*, tr. Chris Turner, (New York: Verso, 1988/1986), 49.

15. Baudrillard, *America*, 87.

16. Baudrillard, *America*, 111.

17. James MacGregor Burns, for example, makes this argument in his book *Leadership* (New York: Harper and Row, 1978).

18. For clarification of the traits of non-voters, see Martin P. Wattenburg, *Where Have All the Voters Gone?* (Cambridge: Harvard University Press, 2002) and/or the classic Richard M. Scrammon and Ben J. Wattenberg, *The Real Majority* (New York: Coward-McCann Publishers, 1970).

19. The appropriate resolution of this disputed election would have been to acknowledge that there was no mechanism within Florida's disgraceful election system to come up with an accurate enough count to declare a winner. The House of

Representatives should have invalidated Florida's electoral vote, throwing the election to Congress. With each state's House delegation getting one vote and with more states Republican than Democratic, the outcome would have been the same—a Bush Presidency—but the process would have been honest rather than fraudulent.

20. Quoted in Peter R. Mitchell and John Schoeffel, eds., *Understanding Power: The Indispensable Chomsky* (New York: The New Press, 2002), 200.

21. Mitchell and Schoeffel, *Understanding Power*, 321–22.

5

A Menace to the World: The American Foreign Policy Environment

The United States professes to be one of the world's foremost champions of democracy and yet, in reality, we have been one of its greatest enemies. Our government has a long and terrible history of overthrowing democratic governments and installing dictatorial, usually fascist, regimes in their place. When, on occasion, we have imposed governments that formally appear representative, closer examination reveals that they were anything but. Our government has also been among the most powerful allies and defenders of many of the world's most hated dictatorships, blocking reform efforts that might well have ushered in democracy. Meanwhile, we as a nation have emerged as a great empire, commanding huge portions of the world's resources and consuming far more per capita than any other nation in the world. The consequence of all of our anti-democratic meddling, attacking, and conquering is an international system of economic and political dominion that secures for American elites a grossly disproportionate share of the world's resource, making poor countries poorer, as well as undemocratic, and making the wealthiest of Americans all the wealthier.

WAR MONGERING: MAKING THE WORLD
SAFE FOR DICTATORSHIP

Among huge segments of the world's population, America is terribly feared and bitterly despised. There are certainly many Americans, especially many neo-conservatives, who are quite happy that the United States is widely feared. In fact, the primary priority among the neo-conservatives who dominated the George W. Bush presidency was to create far more fear of the

United States, especially in the Muslim world, post–9/11. The fatal flaw in this policy direction is that the U.S. military, generally unable to distinguish combatants from non-combatants and certainly unable to separate the two, most readily terrorizes defenseless civilians, especially the very young and the very old who seem least able to get out of harm's way fast enough. Those who are in fact already combatants embracing a violently anti-American ideology of hate are among the most mobile and most difficult to detect and isolate. They have relatively little to fear and, for example, in the case of Islamic fundamentalism, may ascribe to an ideology that reasonably characterizes death at the hands of U.S. forces as being an escape from a hellish Earth and a promotion to a divine Heaven.

The sheer ease with which various Islamist movements have launched wave after wave of suicide bombings should tell even the most dim-witted American foreign policy planner that the problem cannot be solved by creating greater fear with threats of death. Perhaps recent American institutionalization of the use of sexual abuse and torture—best known at Abu Ghraib but in wide use throughout the world—wasn't designed for successful interrogation, for which it fails miserably by compelling fabricated and false confessions among the overwhelmingly innocent as well as a genuine confession among the very rare detainee who really is a terrorist. Perhaps it was designed to impose a fate *worse* than death, for if death is release and salvation, humiliation and agony most certainly are not. The trouble is our use of terror is overwhelmingly victimizing innocents and, as our fairly indiscriminant bombing, shelling, raiding, and torture becomes widely known, as it affects more and more people, and as it leaves in its wake more and more widows and orphans, the merchants of hate who preach anti-Americanism find their sermons are more and more convincing, more obviously true, and more and more successful in eliciting converts and recruits. As a result of this legacy of hatred and the desire for retribution it creates, even we Americans may come to have more and more to fear.

There is nothing new about the use of atrocity in American foreign policy, including genocidal campaigns which claimed the lives of millions of Native Americans and African slaves; bold aggressions starting the Spanish-American and Mexican-American wars, yielding the theft of much of the Caribbean and the better half of Mexico; and the ambitious and abusive colonization of much of the world stretching from the Caribbean, Central and South America all the way to China, the Philippines, and much of the rest of Asia. Where we tend to delude ourselves most, however, is in seeing World War II as our redemption. While it is extremely difficult to find anything defensible in America's military campaigns after the War of Independence, we seem intent on believing that World War II was the critical exception, that it was "the good war."[1] As the story is told in our textbooks and popular culture, it is here where the United States took on the nearly pure evil of the Axis powers and, in so doing, saved the world. What better redemption can a country have? Champions of liberty and self-determination, we saved the world in World War II. No wonder we still seem obsessed with it: movies and documentaries about World War II still occupy huge chunks of our programming time; high school curricula culminate in major units on the war, leaving very little time and attention to all that followed—perhaps a small unit on Vietnam and perhaps another on the Cold War and the fall of Soviet communism, or perhaps not much of either.

However, fighting extraordinary evil does not necessarily make one virtuous. While the goal of defeating Nazi Germany seems an unquestionably worthy one, there is much in the details of how and why America fought that give one pause, that reveal evils of our own, and that refute the notion that this was a "good war" in which we acted selflessly or saved the world.[2] Consider just the following key facets of the war's origins and the conduct that comprised it:

- Far from being initially offended by Nazism, the United States early on fleetingly considered a possible alliance *with* Nazi Germany and was especially interested in a possible joint invasion of the Soviet Union. Stalin's "paranoia" and his forging of a pact with Nazi Germany in an attempt to forestall invasion of the U.S.S.R. were in large measure reactive to American initiatives such as this.
- President Franklin Roosevelt was eager to bring a still isolationist American public into the war and worked very hard to provoke a Japanese attack. Japan preferred a diplomatic solution to the two nations' clash of territorial ambitions in the Pacific. However, American diplomats were instructed to be intentionally rude and uncompromising in an effort to provoke war. Japan had a long history of launching wars via surprise attack and the only real surprise was that the attack came at Hawaii rather than the U.S. controlled Philippines.
- Given America's immediately post–World War II actions aimed at dismantling or preventing democracy (in Vietnam, Korea, Italy, Greece, and elsewhere), our interest in the war may not have been in defending democracy or self-determination. Our goals in the war are better characterized as advancing our ambitions in Asia and defending our investments in Western Europe. Our government even protected our elites' investments in Nazi Germany. For example, the U.S.-based company, Ford Motor Works, manufactured engines, trucks, and automotive parts in Nazi Germany and successfully lobbied the U.S. government postwar for compensation for their factories that were damaged in Allied bombings of Germany.[3]
- Like Nazi Germany, American society at the time was eugenicist and virulently racist. Only American racism can explain why the United States

rounded up Japanese Americans into our own concentration camps but did not do so to German Americans. Our armed forces remained racially segregated and it was African American units that were assigned the worst tasks: for example, the suicidal task of clearing mines from Omaha Beach in advance of the D-Day landing. Of course, racism persists in our re-writing of this history. In Steven Spielberg's *Saving Private Ryan,* the clearing of mines has been expunged; the film depicts in its opening scene of the main D-Day landing, a pristine beach rather than the reality of one littered with the corpses of African American G.I.'s.

- The United States had some complicity in the Holocaust. There was ample American governmental knowledge of the existence of massively genocidal concentration camps in Nazi controlled territory. Human rights advocates urged the U.S. government to bomb the railroad tracks leading to the camps as a way of slowing the slaughter but American officials preferred that the Nazis continue to divert valuable resource from their war effort to run their concentration camps. There was little American governmental concern about the well-being of Jewish and other Holocaust victims.

- The United States government endorsed the British firebombing of Dresden. Widely regarded as the most beautiful and culturally rich city in Europe, Dresden had no real military targets but was wiped out, along with nearly 100,000 civilians, in two nights of firebombing in an effort to deflate German morale. The American firebombing of Tokyo was not all that different.

- America's use of nuclear weapons in Hiroshima and Nagasaki obliterated these two cities. Moreover, these cities were selected because they were "virgin targets," cities that had not suffered significant previous bombing damage because they were of little military significance and preponderantly civilian. However, a primary objective of the U.S. government was to gain better insight into what the new atomic bomb could do. The rush to use nuclear weapons against Japan almost certainly had more to do with preventing the Soviet Union from having time to gain territory to be liberated from the Japanese empire and with securing a purely unconditional surrender than it had to do with the official rationale: the desire to save the lives of American soldiers by making unnecessary an assault on Japan's main islands.[4] Pursuit of a negotiated conditional surrender would have spared the lives of American soldiers and the civilians at Hiroshima and Nagasaki but almost certainly would have been too slow to prevent losses of Japanese territory to the Soviet Union.

Containing and defeating Nazi Germany was certainly a necessary and worthy goal. The key point here, however, is that American foreign policy before, during, and after World War II was motivated and directed by ambitions and methods that were often distressingly similar to those of Nazi Germany.

America does not find any genuine redemption in this history and certainly has not found any since. With victory in the Second World War, the United States emerged as a truly global power with a privileged and imperial presence across the planet. It is in its post–World War II aggressions and manipulations that America's war mongering and anti-democratic malevolences are most obvious. The history of American foreign policy in the post–World War II era is a relentless history of forcefully overthrowing democratic governments, blocking popular movements designed to introduce democracy, violently imposing upon other countries dictatorial (usually fascist) regimes, installing in other nations false democracies (governments that at first glance seem formally representative but, in reality, systemically disempower majorities of the population), and militarily, politically, and economically defending dictatorial allies, insulating them against domestic and international pressure to democratize.

Though challenged and confronted by the Soviet Union from time to time, since World War II America has had no equal. Our foreign policy reach was and remains truly global, and our initiatives have been malevolent, dictatorial, and imperial. Even our government has acknowledged this. Following the many governmental crimes and abuses of the Watergate scandal and of the related misuse of power by the Nixon administration (which included misuse of the Central Intelligence Agency), Congress launched a full scale investigation of CIA activities from the end of World War II to the time of the investigation, 1975. The Senate Committee on Intelligence, the Church Committee named for Senator Frank Church, issued the Grimmett Report.[5] Based on subpoenaed CIA documents, it confirmed what many scholars had long suspected: the U.S. government had repeatedly toppled democracies, imposed and defended dictatorships, and blocked democratic reform movements around the globe.

There have been many government confirmed American overthrows of democratic governments: Iran in 1953, Guatemala in 1954, both the Congo and Ecuador in 1961, Greece in 1967, and Chile in 1973. In all of these cases, the CIA supplanted a democratic government in order to impose a brutal dictatorship. In 1953, the CIA toppled the democratic and popular government of Iranian Prime Minister Mohammad Mossadegh. Mossadegh had led a very popular initiative to nationalize the British owned oil company that monopolized oil production and sales in Iran. The nationalization bill was supported overwhelmingly in the Iranian parliament but the United States endorsed the British desire to get rid of Mossadegh's democracy and launched a CIA directed coup d'etat that brought absolute dictatorial powers to the then figurehead monarch, Shah Mohammed Reza

Pahlavi. Following CIA directives, the Shah fired Mossadegh and replaced him with General Fazollah Zahedi, a wartime Nazi collaborator. Mossadegh resisted as mass demonstrations came to his aid and the Shah fled to Rome in fear. However, the CIA campaign persisted—spreading disinformation, buying mobs, bribing members of Parliament, and eventually launching military intervention—and the Shah was persuaded to return to lead what quickly emerged as an absolutist dictatorship which terrorized, imprisoned, and tortured dissenters for twenty-five years. Mossadegh was imprisoned for three years and then placed under house arrest until his death. The United States probably inadvertently created far more than it bargained for: it was overwhelming hatred for the Shah's regime and hatred of the United States for imposing and supporting it, that led to the world's first successful Islamist revolution in 1978, the full effects of which we have not yet witnessed.

In 1954, the United States forcefully overthrew the democratic government of Guatemala, led at the time by Socialist President Jacobo Arbenz, who was easily elected in 1951 on a political platform calling for land reform and improved unionization rights for workers. Not wanting to risk having to pay higher wages, United Fruit Corporation, better known by the name of its Chiquita product line, called upon the Eisenhower administration to get rid of Arbenz's government. The U.S. government agreed to do so, and the CIA engineered a military coup that ousted democracy in the country, sent Arbenz into an itinerant life of exile, and introduced a brutal military dictatorship that consistently ranked among Amnesty International's top handful of human rights abusers. All told, roughly 200,000 were killed, many of whom "disappeared" to torture and death. The U.S. government denied its actions then but many conservatives now defend them on the grounds that among Arbenz's supporters in Guatemala's legislature was the country's tiny communist party. Such a view ignores Arbenz's staunchly anti-communist positions at the U.N. and at home. Besides, many neo-Nazi groups have endorsed Republicans in America; that hardly means that the Republican Party is fascist or that its elected officials can be legitimately overthrown by force. Even when civilian rule was restored in Guatemala as a formal technicality in the 1980s, extraordinary power remained and remains with the army—so much so that one civilian President, Fernando Romeo Lucas Garcia, publicly admitted that the army would kill him if he diverged very far from their wishes. Guatemala's military began to lose dominance in the 1990s, but the country remains at the mercy of one of the more abusive and corrupt regimes in the world.

The CIA also played the pivotal role in ordering and orchestrating the assassination of populist black nationalist Patrice Lumumba, the first Prime Minister of Congo (first called the Belgian Congo, then the Congo, later Zaire, and now the Congo again). He was elected with a plurality of votes in Congo's first post-independence elections in 1960. Unlike Mossadegh and

Arbenz, Lumumba did eventually develop ties with the Soviet Union when, trying to expel Belgian troops supporting a secessionist Katanga province, he was rebuffed by the U.N. and the United States and could only find military aid from the U.S.S.R. The Church committee concluded that U.S. Secretary of State, Allen Dulles himself, ordered Lumumba's assassination. In the wake of the power vacuum created by Lumumba's murder, the CIA supported both the dictatorially inclined Mobutu Sese Seko, who was directly involved in Lumumba's murder, and the more moderate Cyrille Adoula. It was Mobutu who would eventually prevail and rule the country for thirty-two years of dictatorship and extraordinary looting of the nation's resources.

In 1960, Ecuador elected as president the liberal politician José María Velasco Ibarra. The American government was greatly displeased by his refusal to break ties with Cuba and to ban communist parties. The CIA began a campaign aimed at triggering a military coup: bombing right-wing organizations, ridiculing the army, and attributing these actions to liberals and leftists. The military forced President Velasco to resign in November of 1961, manipulated his successor, and staged a full-scale military take-over in 1963. As a result, communism was outlawed, many leftists and liberals imprisoned (along with their families and friends), and full scale military dictatorship arose, persisting until 1979.

The CIA also orchestrated a military coup in Greece several days before elections that would have returned liberal George Papandreou to the Prime Ministership. Although Papandreou was a proven anti-communist, his son Andreas, who seemed certain to figure prominently in the new administration, had openly criticized Greece's membership in NATO and seriously alarmed American foreign policy makers as a result. The CIA hand-picked as leader of the new military junta Colonel Georgios Papadopoulos who was selected for two key reasons: first, he had worked for the CIA for many years, and second, the CIA alone knew that he had been an important collaborator with the Nazis, knowledge which guaranteed that he would remain subject to CIA control. Of course, given that control, the seven year long Greek junta's extensive use of torture to terrorize Greeks into submission is something for which the United States bears full responsibility.

In 1970, Chileans elected as president a socialist, Salvador Allende. In order to avoid possible nationalization of their holdings, International Telephone & Telegraph (ITT) moved quickly to persuade the Nixon administration to take action to keep Allende from taking office. A full scale political destabilization campaign was launched, but most effective in undermining the new President's popularity was a suspension of aid and an economic embargo. By 1973, Allende's party nonetheless made significant gains in legislative elections, and Allende advanced a plan calling for the nationalization of ITT and Anaconda Copper holdings. The two American-based companies were to be reimbursed for their full value as stated on their

Chilean tax returns. Since the companies had been cheating on their taxes for many years, grossly understating their true value, this left them in an embarrassing position—admit their fraud to demand a fair price or accept gross underpayment for their assets—and subsequently, quite angry. They thus called upon Nixon to direct the CIA to take far more forceful action, which it did. The ensuing military coup ended democracy in Chile and brought to power a fascist military junta headed by General Augusto Pinochet. Allende was killed in the coup, either murdered in the onslaught upon the Presidential Palace or, as the Pinochet dictatorship claimed and later exhumation and autopsy seemed to confirm, a suicide in order to avoid the former fate.[6] Most of those who worked closely with the Allende government were rounded up and killed. U.S. Secretary of State Henry Kissinger has been accused of facilitating and encouraging some of these murders by providing the Pinochet junta with the names and Chilean home addresses of American citizens, mostly young adults, who went to Chile to work with the Allende government. The CIA had done something very similar in Indonesia in 1965, providing the emerging Suharto dictatorship, which orchestrated campaigns that killed hundreds of thousands, the names and addresses of thousands of "communist" Indonesians. Kissinger's alleged death lists were much, much smaller, but this allegation of Kissinger's involvement was far worse in the sense that conspiracy to murder *American* citizens might be considered a crime under U.S. law and not just yet another *international* crime for which there are no real legal repercussions. However, the U.S. government declined to investigate. The Pinochet dictatorship lasted, in various forms, for roughly two decades, all with U.S. support—a very sad but all too common history of American manufactured and sponsored political repression, disappearances, torture, and murder.

Not all CIA efforts to overthrow democracies have succeeded. The American government twice tried to overthrow the presidency of José Figueres in Costa Rica, first in 1955 and then again in 1970 to 1971. Without a Congressional investigation and a new Grimmett style report covering the period since 1975, it is impossible to know for sure what evils the CIA has been up to in more recent decades. But, given the rapidity with which President George W. Bush acknowledged and embraced a new military regime in the initial hours of the failed 2002 coup attempt against Venezuelan President Hugo Chavez, it seems a reasonable guess that the CIA was involved and disappointed that a popular uprising by both military and civilian populations quickly reversed the course of the coup. Chavez is almost certainly much less democratic than the leaders discussed above. Although he came to power and remains there largely because of his success in elections, he has increasingly modified the country's constitution to give himself more autocratic powers and longer and longer tenure in the presidency. To depose another

Latin-American quasi-dictatorial President, Daniel Ortega, who headed the hybrid anarchist-communist Sandinista Party in Nicaragua, required the United States to organize, fund, and direct a counter-revolutionary army, the Contras, for the better part of the 1980s. In the Iran-Contra scandal, the Reagan administration defied a Congressional ban on this war mongering by illegally and secretly channeling money and weapons to the Contras via Islamist Iran of all places. Many years of American initiated and sponsored war eventually succeeded in pressuring the Sandinistas into signing a peace deal returning elections to the country. This allowed the CIA to pour millions into the campaign treasuries of rightist candidates to help secure their election. However, Ortega finally returned to the presidency, this time via election, in 2006.

One of the more tragic repercussions of America's anti-democratic initiatives may be this: it is precisely those leaders who are most democratic who are most vulnerable to CIA engineered coups and those leftists who are willing to resort to more autocratic (Chavez) or even dictatorial (Fidel Castro in communist Cuba) measures who are safest, and who generally best survive American plots against their lives and governments. In this manner, America encourages anti-democratic governance where it fails, as well as where it succeeds.

Imposition of American determined government upon other countries has not always required a special CIA operation or American military invasion dedicated to that goal. The liberation of territories from imperial Japan at the end of World War II offered the United States a unique opportunity to choose governments for other peoples. The anti-democratic decisions America made in Korea and Vietnam not only cost the lives of millions of Asians, via political repression as well as subsequent warfare, but eventually also cost over 120,000 American soldiers their lives as well.

Neither the Korean nor Vietnam wars were simply matters of defending non-communist states from communist invasion. In Korea, as Japan was defeated, the government of the American-seized-South was as much dictated by America as the government of the Soviet-seized-North was by the U.S.S.R. It was very telling that the United States set up in South Korea a military government, aligned it with far right, kept the Japanese occupation system intact (including the use of a brutal secret police), and used a campaign of murder and terror to crush political moderates and leftists. By 1946, America had placed in charge of southern Korea ultra-rightists and the ultra-nationalist dictator, Syngmon Rhee. The reign of terror Rhee imposed killed about 50,000 people, thus undermining the credibility of American claims that defending South Korea was defending democracy or self-determination. When North Korea did make incursions into South Korea, the United States sought not merely to repel the incursions but to conquer the North as well. Americans may have seized defeat from apparent victory by bringing U.S. troops so close to China, by bombing as far north as the border bridges over the Yalu River and, in the process, almost certainly hitting Manchuria itself on several different occassions. The resulting Chinese counter-attack, which brought them into the war, was truly massive and caused the war to end in an eventual stalemate.

In Vietnam at the end of World War II, Ho Chi Minh and his nationalist supporters had initially won the blessing of the United States, but France persuaded America to renege on its promises of support and to sanction French re-conquest of their former colony. Even the release of Japanese prisoners of war for help in the subjugation of Vietnam and the creation and imposition of a French controlled dictatorial government in the South was sanctioned by the United States. Despite American propaganda to the contrary, preponderant Vietnamese popular opinion throughout Vietnam, both North and South, remained with Ho (even as, out of necessity, he turned to the Soviet Union and China for support) and favored reunification.

The United States actively undermined the 1954 Geneva Accords, the end of the French phase of the war, by introducing American advisors and troops to try to sustain the French-created and imposed puppet state of South Vietnam. Perhaps an even more telling American departure from the Geneva Accords was breaking the promise to resolve the conflict with a national referendum to determine the question of reunification. The United States argued, unconvincingly, that no assurances could guarantee the absence of voting fraud in and by the North. However, it was abundantly apparent that no American efforts were made to negotiate a monitored election process and that American policymakers were keenly aware that anything approaching a democratic election would result in reunification of the country under Ho's leadership.

Democracy was, in this way, a major threat to the American position in Vietnam; democratic self-determination would almost certainly lead to reunification of the country, a single communist Vietnam. Hence, for the United States, democracy in Vietnam was something that must be avoided. America's South Vietnam ally was extremely dictatorial and corrupt; in the case of Ngo Dinh Diem, it was so corrupt that the CIA murderously ousted him. Despite a brief interlude of anti-American civilian rule, South Vietnam was governed by a series of military-led puppet governments. The fascist, undemocratic, and brutal nature of these puppets of America spoke volumes about America's hostility to democracy in Vietnam. The National Liberation Front (NLF), or Vietcong, was comprised of southerners fighting *for* national reunification during the American phase of the war. The NLF enjoyed massive support throughout South Vietnam and they offered a majority of the daily resistance to the American occupation of the country. Democracy in South Vietnam was an oxymoron. This may have been a good part of the reason why the Vietnam War was particularly ugly. American soldiers were placed in the untenable position of trying to subdue nearly the entirety of a heavily populated rural country. Indiscriminant attacks with anti-personnel and defoliant weaponry and the routine annihilation of villagers, most extreme at My Lai but a daily occurrence on a smaller scale, were perhaps inevitable given this situation. So was failure.

Where America hasn't been overturning democracy it has often blocked its emergence. For example, in the 1950s, the United States delayed the independence of its own colony, the Philippines, and later blocked reform minded candidates from taking office after being democratically elected. The CIA even drugged presidential candidate Elpedo Quirino so he would appear incoherent delivering a public speech and lose the election. A military coup was planned in the event that he somehow won anyway. In 1964, the United States persuaded Great Britain to delay British Guiana's independence in order to block the democratically elected Dr. Cheddi Jagan from taking office. In 1965, U.S. Marines invaded the Dominican Republic to put down a popular uprising aiming to restore democracy to the country and bring back to office socialist Juan Bosch, who had been ousted in a military coup nineteen months earlier.

Where America hasn't blocked democracy per se, it has often meddled in its processes and manipulated its outcomes. The most famous examples here may be Australia in the late '60s and early '70s, when the CIA channeled millions of dollars to the Liberal Party in a failed effort to help it defeat the Labor Party;[7] and Jamaica in the late '70s, when the CIA orchestrated a full political and economic destabilization campaign as it channeled millions of dollars to the Jamaica Labour Party, in a successful effort to help it defeat People's National Party Prime Minister, Michael Manley.

America has quite often supported and defended many of the world's least democratic regimes, and the whole point of toppling and blocking democracies has been to maximize American control and exploitation of other nations. A list of America's key allies in this history features many regimes that were or remain terrible: Haiti, El Salvador, apartheid South Africa, Taiwan, Saudi Arabia, Egypt, and Israel (oppressive not toward its own citizens but toward Palestinians living under perpetual martial law in perpetually occupied territories); these are just a few of those not already discussed above. Often it was only the intercession of American troops or the provision of American weapons that allowed these regimes to exist or to be as bad as they were.

In recent decades, the United States appears to be more adept at creating false democracies: regimes that are structured in a seemingly democratic way but whose policies and actual processes of power are mostly inconsistent with genuine democracy. Such may be the case in Grenada, where the United

States invaded in 1986 to oust a communist government only to insert a "democracy" where all leftist parties and leftist labor organizations were banned. Of course, there was much that was suspicious about this invasion: how closely it followed the embarrassment of the Beirut barracks bombing that killed 241 American soldiers supporting the Christian government in Lebanon's civil war (Was the Grenada invasion an attempt to divert attention away from a foreign policy debacle?); how hard the Reagan administration worked to implausibly claim that American students might be taken hostage (If there was plenty of opportunity before the U.S. invasion for American students in Grenada to be taken hostage and it didn't happen, then what was the real motivation for the U.S. invasion?); and how grossly incompetent the American invasion was (Why did it take nearly a week for the U.S. military to defeat a small island with only a minuscule number of soldiers?). In the context of these circumstances and questions, it certainly makes sense to wonder if the CIA may have had a role in instigating the communist party infighting that led to President Maurice Bishop's murder and precipitated the "crisis" that the United States used to rationalize its invasion.

In recent years, the United States hasn't overthrown as many democracies as was its practice earlier. Indeed, in the post–Cold War world, America has increasingly directed its aggressions against Islamic societies, which, because of poverty, tend not to have democratic governments to begin with. Still, false democracy may be America's true preference and it may be a very apt description of the new American-created governments in Afghanistan and Iraq. How can America's choice in Afghanistan, the heavily backed presidency of Hamid Karzai, be considered democratic when Karzai doesn't even fully govern the capital city of Kabul and defers to his allies of warlords (drug dealers, extortionists, and thugs) to have some means of containing Taliban resurgence in the preponderance of the country? How can the electoral system of Iraq be considered democratic when the 2005 elections were held with grossly inadequate preparation; when Sunni communities were still devastated by ongoing warfare, continuous lack of water and electricity, and failure to repair any significant portion of the devastation caused by American bombing; when there were no accurate census figures available; when ethnic and religious militias intimidated much of the population (especially Sunnis); and when political party lists were identified by religious symbols conveying not political platforms but only ethnic and sectarian affiliation?[8] Try to imagine an American election wherein districts that lean toward one particular party are under military siege and extreme depravation while votes are being collected. With what audacity are Americans willing to label an Iraqi equivalent of that scenario "democratic"?

Americans seem to have little awareness of what transpired in the American wars against Afghanistan (largely forgotten because of low *American* death tolls) and against Iraq (largely unpopular but only because of its longevity and the high cost to the lives of American soldiers and to the U.S. treasury). Motivated not by any genuine desire to export democracy but rather by a desire to terrorize much of the Islamic world in response to 9/11, America's true goals in Afghanistan and Iraq are not what most Americans think that they are.

With regard to Afghanistan, the U.S. government never demonstrated, or even made any systematic attempt to try to demonstrate, that Al Qaeda was in fact responsible for, or participatory in, the September 11 attacks.[9] Instead, Osama bin Laden and Al Qaeda were singled out as something like "the usual suspect" *assumed* by most everyone to be responsible. The Taliban regime refused to assist the United States in its efforts to eliminate Al Qaeda but they did so with full awareness that an American invasion to oust them was inevitable, that the American policymakers were determined to instill fear in the Islamic world and an anti-Taliban invasion was coming whether or not they chose a path of appeasement. Meanwhile, the United States itself has been intransigent in refusing the call of others to bring terrorists to justice. For example, America provides safe refuge for many anti-Cuba terrorists. Most notorious among many is Orlando Bosch who committed many terrorists attacks against Cuba, including the 1976 bombing of a Cuban airplane, which killed 73 passengers.

Furthermore, American "successes" in the war have been grossly exaggerated. The American deal to get Pakistan to switch from supporting the Taliban to opposing them involved guaranteeing the airlifting of Pakistani soldiers, and with America's initial efforts focused on safely extricating the Pakistani army from Afghanistan, the Taliban were given time to disperse in advance of the obviously ensuing U.S. bombing and invasion. The American government has grossly overestimated Taliban deaths and grossly underestimates civilian ones, especially because of extensive, indiscriminant cluster bombing. American soldiers have either met ferocious resistance or zero engagement but, by far, it has been mostly the latter, allowing the Taliban time to regroup and recruit.[10]

American efforts in Afghanistan have been, and continue to be, seriously undermined by the unsavory character of key allies. In the war's early phases, there was fear among American strategists that dispersal of the Taliban would allow our new and disreputable ally, the Northern Alliance, to rush into Kabul where it was feared that they would launch a bloodbath against civilians. Later, the United States pasted together for Karzai a fragile alliance of corrupt warlords, but banditry and the drug trade may be what is best thriving in Afghanistan these days, while the Taliban resistance, though still small scale, is little weaker. For a war that gets little attention here, America may be well on its way to losing it anyway. Besides, how wise was it for America to approve Pakistan's possession of nuclear weapons, part of the deal to get Pakistan to switch sides, in order to try to kill 50,000 Taliban soldiers, given the unpopularity and instability of the Pakistani dictatorship and the growing threat of an Islamist revolution there? Is fake democracy in Afghanistan adequate recompense for genuine dictatorship in Pakistan?

As for Iraq, the American rationale for going to war there was in the final analysis baseless. Iraq did *not* possess, and was not attempting to possess, weapons of mass destruction. In fact, the Bush administration went to enormous lengths to justify this war by creating a "threat" out of whole cloth.[11] While it is true that Saddam Hussein was a tyrant, the tyrannical quality of many of America's key and heavily subsidized allies in the war (such as Islam Karimov in Uzbekistan or Pervez Musharraf in Pakistan) is, by almost any objective measure, far worse. Musharraf's government than probably killed many more civilians than Hussein's regime did and Karimov's dictatorship is among world's most active torturers of suspected dissidents, with the repulsive practice of boiling victims' limbs or whole selves as the preferred method of torture and execution. Was it that Hussein was considered a menace less for the scope of his tyranny and more for the territorial ambitions he exhibited with his 1990 invasion of Kuwait, which prompted the first Gulf War? That's unlikely. Iraq's invasion of Kuwait was motivated as much or more by an oil dispute than by territorial ambition. Corrupt and petty Kuwait was rapidly pumping oil from an enormous oil pool, which lies preponderantly in Iraq, and refused to negotiate any compromise. American Ambassador to Iraq, April Glaspie, promised Hussein that the United States would do nothing but complain about an invasion of Kuwait, perhaps luring him into a trap to provide an excuse for warring with Iraq. In any event, the United States refused Hussein's many attempts to negotiate withdrawal from Kuwait in return for an American promise not to attack. Given Israel's longstanding complaints about the growth of Hussein's army, it seems most likely that Israel convinced the United States that the size of Iraq's army at the time was a threat and that the real goal of the first American Gulf War was to decimate that army. That was the war's outcome (although, contrary to our propaganda, even more Iraqi civilians than soldiers were killed), and our purported key allies suffered greatly to provide it: Kuwait may have unnecessarily endured a brutal Iraqi invasion and protracted occupation, and Iraq's Shiites and Kurds, who had been promised American help if they rebelled against Hussein, were left for slaughter upon the withdrawal of American troops.

In advance of America's 2003 invasion, Iraq was well contained militarily, without weapons of mass destruction of any kind (having dismantled even the chemical weapons the United States provided when, following Israel's lead, it wished to try to extend the Iran-Iraq War by helping whichever side was at the time losing); it was thus incapable of menacing any neighbor, let alone other states, in any significant way. Hussein had never been anything but hostile to Islamic fundamentalism and groups like Al Qaeda.

So what was the real purpose of the invasion? Perhaps, above all, the American invasion of Iraq was intended to spread fear of America throughout the Islamic world by targeting a country more meaningful and sizable than Afghanistan but still seemingly vulnerable in a war that would be manageable.

Unfortunately for the United States, the effectiveness of massive bombing was undermined by the dispersal of Iraqi troops prior to the bombardment (the Iraqi army was directed to bring themselves, their weapons, and their ammunition to their homes prior to the American attacks). While penetrating the country was remarkable easy, actually controlling or managing it has been remarkably difficult, especially as the war has devolved into a sectarian civil war with most Shiites and Kurds generally supporting the American established new government and most Sunnis comprising the heart of many of the resistance movements. The key factor here is that people are being killed on the basis of their sectarian affiliation, and individuals often have little choice but to cast their lot with their sectarian community. Given this, there is little prospect that such a war can be truly resolved in any direction anytime soon. The intensity of hostility in Iraq has been made much worse by American mismanagement. Beginning with the 2003 invasion, the American occupation of Iraq was run as one might expect: as an absolutist dictatorship managed by the occupying force. However, what is distressing if not fully surprising is that American policymakers in Iraq essentially ignored the most pressing Iraqi needs and concerns: the need to rebuild, to restore water and electricity, to pay Iraqi employees, and, probably most critical of all, to begin to meaningfully address the security needs of Iraqi civilians. Instead, the United States pursued a strangely irrelevant and neo-conservative ideological agenda of privatization, ending import duties, and introducing a flat tax. Meanwhile, rabid de-Baathification (the purging of those connected with Hussein's party and government) seriously undermined the more critical American goals of building viable Iraqi military and police forces. When added to the obvious corruption lining the pockets of American corporate officials, the indiscriminant violence of the U.S. military and private American "security" firms, and the lavish luxuries for Americans walled within the Green Zone, the United States quickly alienated even those who might have welcomed a restructuring of Iraq.[12]

With lulls or not, a great many years of war, seem inevitable, and it is perhaps all but certain that the United States will not be willing to stay for very much more of it. Sadly, the legacy America will leave to those who will continue the civil war in Iraq is a false democracy that is unlikely to last very long and the precedents of using widespread torture (at Abu Ghraib and elsewhere) and using a chemical weapon of mass destruction, white phosphorus (which seems to meet the Geneva Accord's definitional criteria of a chemical weapon but which the United States wants stubbornly to deny).

In the war begun over an American panic about weapons of mass destruction, only the United States had them and, most ironic of all, we used them.

In this disturbing history of America's post–World War II warring and military manipulations, if the sheer frequency and duration of warfare isn't daunting enough, the overwhelmingly anti-democratic nature of American initiatives is. Although the devil is often in the details, such as the heinous nature of intentionally selecting former Nazi collaborators as dictators for other nations, journalist and former Foreign Service Officer William Blum has aptly summed up the toll of American foreign policy brutalities this way:

> From 1945 to 2003, the United States attempted to overthrow more than 40 foreign governments, and to crush more than 30 populist-nationalist movements fighting against intolerable regimes. In the process, the US bombed some 25 countries, caused the end of life for several million people, and condemned many millions more to a life of agony and despair.[13]

The more precise effects of American foreign policy malevolence vary from nation to nation. Where the Left has been destroyed by years of American initiatives dating back to the Cold War, anti-American violence and hatred explodes from the Right with anti-minority nationalisms, authoritarian populisms, and aspirations of war with the United States. Where the Right is weaker (for example, where Islamic fundamentalism has few Muslims to call upon), new leftist political movements still focus on land reform, resource access, and indigenous rights, and they call upon the perhaps timeless traditions of socialism, communism, anarchism, and populism.[14] In either setting, America has truly become, and is seen as, a menace to the world.

How can a country like ours, which pays such lip service to democratic values, be so consistently dismantling those values abroad? How can a pluralist government so limited in its abilities to change America, so easily be toying with the destinies and fates of other nations? In part, the answer lies in the nature of our constitution, which has been interpreted consistently as protecting only *our* citizenry from our government. It offers no protection for the peoples of other countries. In part too, maybe it is all the weakness our politicians endure domestically that provokes a hyperactive effort to prove their strength overseas. Is it the emasculated who are most likely to avoid equals and beat the defenseless? Is it our own sense of internal weakness that encourages a false sense of our moral superiority over the rest of the world and leads us to treat all those who even resemble those that frighten us, communists in the past and Islamists now, with impunity and a cruel indifference to their perspectives, wants, and needs? But perhaps something even more nefarious is at work here: Is "the American way of

life" tied in any way to these abuses of weaker nations? Are we an empire?
Do we thrive on repression and manipulation?

THE NEW IMPERIALISM: THE REVERSE
ROBIN HOOD ON A GLOBAL SCALE

The United States has become preponderantly a nation of service providers: salesmen, healthcare providers of one sort or another, educators, wait staff, lawyers, engineers, and so on. Yet this country in which hardly anyone *makes* anything (that is, creates a tangible product) is populated by people who *consume* a disproportionately large share of the world's goods and resources—more than most anywhere else in the world. How is it that a country that produces so little consumes so much? Ultimately, it is impossible to answer this question without coming to terms with the role of power in international relations and the ways in which malevolent American foreign policy has been geared toward securing other peoples' resources cheaply and often against their will. In short, the upshot of all the attacking and conquering in American foreign policy has been to secure a disproportionate share of the world's resource, making poor countries poorer, Americans richer, and the wealthiest of Americans even wealthier.

America has indeed become an empire. Unlike the old Roman or British empires of bygone years, the new imperialism, or neo-imperialism, no longer requires the expense of formal colonization and constant military occupation. To be sure, we have already seen that America has not been shy about resorting to many military invasions and takeovers of one sort or another. But, on a daily basis, international imperialism runs less on military domination and more on manipulations of markets, prices, trade and shipping routes, loan availability and rates, repayment schedules, and the like. Even when U.S. military intervention is not threatened, many poor and weak countries have reason to fear America. As the many leaders of poor nations have complained, the only thing worse than being exploited by the United States is not being exploited by the United States. To be isolated from the global economy, even when that economy is so easily dominated by very wealthy countries, is impoverishing in its own right. This is not to say that imperial exploitation is acceptable behavior. For example, American women are probably far better off being exploited in both the workplace and the home than they were when exploited only in the home and excluded from the paid work force, as was prevalently the case prior to the mid-to-late 20th century. Yet who but the worst of chauvinists would argue that it is therefore permissible to engage in misogynist wage discrimination now? The facility with which many privileged Americans will make essentially the same argument about exploiting the third world, that it is fine to exploit these nations because they would suffer even more by being excluded from international trade, is tantamount to demanding lower wages for women for the above stated reasons and is profoundly disturbing, in this regard.

There are many ways to get a general sense of the scope of American imperialism. Perhaps the easiest is to make a quick and rough mental inventory of the sorts of things the typical American owns and consumes: an automobile (and gasoline), appliances, electronics, furniture, clothing, footwear, food, and any number of other simple products. Of these, only furniture and food is produced mostly or, at least, very largely in the United States. Automobiles come mostly from Japan, South Korea, Mexico, and other countries. Even American brand car companies like Ford or General Motors are mostly just *assembling* foreign-made parts in the United States. "Our" oil (and we consume roughly a quarter of the world's supply) comes mostly from the Middle East, Africa, and Venezuela. Appliances are now made largely in Mexico. Electronics still come mostly from South Korea, Japan, and other Asian nations. Clothing production is dominated by nations with relatively cheap labor: Bangladesh, Indonesia, Malaysia, and Vietnam. Shoes come largely from Brazil and sneakers from Vietnam. Even "our" furniture and food supply are becoming increasingly and extensively foreign based: for example, furniture from China; bananas, sugar, and most of "our" illegal drugs from Latin America; coffee from Latin America and Africa; chocolate from Africa; and so on.

Another way to think about American consumption of the world's resource is to look at our international annual trade deficit, the extent to which the amount of goods and services Americans purchase from non-Americans exceeds the amount of goods and services Americans sell to non-Americans. In 2007, the annual trade deficit was roughly $700 billion, nearly $2,400 *per* American. There are many economists who are worried about the scope of this deficit and note with alarm that it enables foreigners to purchase and own more and more of American enterprises. However, this deficit is also reflective of the strength of the United States; it is indicative of the ability of Americans to command much of the world's resource and exploit much of its labor force. For the most part, the trade deficit *under*states American imperialism because U.S. military and economic power is used to keep third world resources available and *under*compensated. Typically, what we buy is worth more than what our companies pay to extract it and would cost a lot more if international laborers were paid and treated decently. What our companies sell to other nations is similarly *over*valued, and so the trade deficit figure significantly falls short of revealing the full magnitude of American imperialism.

Yet another way to look at American imperialism is by estimating our ecological footprint—in other words, how much land and water area is required to produce what we consume and absorb the waste we generate (the average American generates nearly 60 tons of garbage in a lifetime) under prevailing technological conditions. Globally, humanity is over-stressing the planet. It now takes 14 months for the earth to produce what our species uses in 12 months. Obviously, this cannot persist indefinitely. We will need some combination of technological revolution and consumption control to avert eventual disaster. Of course, we make great technological strides all the time, but lately they haven't been of sufficiently enormous magnitude to compensate for even greater increases in resource depletion. And it should not be surprising that the true masters of over-consumption are Americans. The average American annually consumes what now requires 24 acres to produce, and yet the United States, even with its extraordinary resource and technology, is now only capable of producing about 12 acres of resource per American. As a result, our ecological footprint is about minus 12 acres per American. Seen from this vantage point, the cost of about half of our way of life is imposed upon other parts of the world, and if everyone on the planet now lived like the typical American, we would need 5 and a quarter Earths to sustain it.[15] Ecological footprints are not designed to be indices of imperialism. Some of the poorest nations in the world have negative ecological footprints not because they consume so much but, rather, because they are capable of producing so little. For wealthy nations, however, an ecological footprint serves as a very useful measure of excess. It takes profound and growing inequities in resource distribution and worrisome stresses on the planet's capacities to sustain America's current levels of consumption and considering the foreign origins of so much of what we consume, the sheer magnitude of importation, and the hyperactive malevolence of our foreign policy, it hard to deny that America is an imperial power.

It is often very easy to see imperial motivations in our foreign policy. For example, how can one make sense of United Fruit Company's role in instigating the CIA coup against Arbenz in Guatemala without thinking about cheap bananas and high corporate profits from them? How can one think about the CIA engineered coup against Mossadegh in Iran without thinking about cheap oil? How can one reflect on the role of U.S. corporations in promoting Pinochet's ouster of Allende in Chile without thinking again about imperialism as a source of American foreign policy? The flip side of the continued manipulation and exploitation of nations such as these is the ongoing poverty and misery that is pervasive there. This is the fundamental truth inherent in dependency theory: the wealth of the first world is directly connected to the poverty of the third world. Each makes the other a reality.

Aside from corporate activities and government military incursions, even American "foreign aid" and loan policy is an instrument of exploitation. Former business consultant John Perkins has written a very readable account of his career as an "economic hit man." Perkins' former career involved writing intentionally and grossly optimistic forecasts of various third world countries' anticipated growth. The purpose of these "forecasts" was to secure very large U.S. government endorsed loans. With American corporations grossly overcharging third world nations for nearly all development projects, much if not most of the money from these loans went, in the form of profits, to U.S. corporations securing contracts from the poor nations, and, in the form of kickbacks, to the corrupt indigenous elites who did business with them. The country itself, its people, were left burdened by massive debt—something very useful to the U.S. government seeking to be relatively more certain of the poor nation's malleability, since heavily indebted countries are generally easier to manipulate.[16] The inequity of all this is rather mind-boggling. Loans are issued in the name of an entire poor country but huge portions of the money are siphoned off as profits by American corporations and corrupt native elites. Often these elites were foisted upon a poor nation by an American sponsored military coup. These corrupt elites then left the burden of this massive debt for future generations of ordinary poor citizens, who benefited little if at all from the initial loan and yet must continue to struggle to repay it. Refusal to repay, cancellation of debts occasionally championed by independent minded third world politicians, is one of the most certain triggers of additional American military intervention.

Where does all this leave the third world? It certainly leaves it much poorer than it need be. More than ten million a year die from hunger-related causes. Even when not directly related to hunger, lack of sanitation and of clean water and want of the most rudimentary vaccines and medical treatments adds dramatically to the annual toll. Think of it: each and every year there are completely unnecessary deaths beyond the magnitude of the entire Nazi Holocaust—all largely because of the global neo-imperialism of which the United States is the primary architect.

Beyond the death toll, there are the many fold more populations of those who work in squalid conditions for a pittance. One-sixth of the world's population live on one dollar or less per day and nearly half live on two dollars or less a day. Tens of millions are actually enslaved—unpaid and at the mercy of their owners—for example, Thailand's "prostitutes," often female children, primarily "servicing" westerners, including Americans; Ghana's and the Ivory Coast's young boys who farm cocoa to be consumed mostly here and in capitalist Western Europe; and countless "domestic servants" who go owned and unpaid throughout much of the first world, including the United States.[17]

The third world outbursts of resentment, anger, nationalism, and retaliation, which most Americans are quick to label "terrorist" and/or "extremist," are better understood as the logical consequences of imposing and maintaining an empire. The world's leftists are certainly correct that there is sufficient resource in the world such that, if it was distributed more equitably rather than siphoned off so extensively by and for Americans and many other Westerners, we should be able to eliminate the lion's share of the world's suffering. The surge in Islamic fundamentalism's popularity is due not only to American and Western excesses but also due to a realization that Godliness (not generally defined in pacifist ways) may be our best behavior and Heaven our best reward. Americans are renowned not for any sense of justice, virtue, or fair play; instead, American "culture," especially in its mass media expressions, seems to be continuously celebrating our apparent national pastimes of drinking and whoring. For obvious reasons, these are not generally considered virtues in the Islamic world, which can perhaps reasonably feel superior at least in its relative lack of perverse hedonisms. From both the left and the right, however, there is a world of anti-Americanism out there. From both quarters, it is both reasoned and logical. The realities of American exploitation and excess support anti-Americanism's legitimacy and persuasiveness. The better part of the world is eager for America to fall and, if need be, they stand ready to give a good hardy push.

NOTES

1. For a good general and fairly tame critique of the notion that World War II was "the good war," see Michael C. C. Adams, *The Best War Ever: America and World War II* (Baltimore: Johns Hopkins University Press, 1994). More substantive details about the unsavory aspect of America's conduct in World War II can be found in two very general overviews of the history of the time period: Howard Zinn, *A People's History of the United States 1492–Present* (New York: Perennial Classics, 2001), 407–42 and William Chafe, *The Unfinished Journey: America Since World War II*, 5th ed. (New York: Oxford University Press, 2003), 3–30.

2. Portions of the descriptions of America's modern wars that follow in this chapter first appeared in my article, "No Good Wars: Teaching the History of Modern Wars as a Means of Resisting Current Ones," *College Teaching* 55, no. 2 (Winter 2008): 1–7. I wish to thank Heldref Publications for allowing them to appear here.

3. See Charles Higham, *Trading with the Enemy: An Exposé of the Nazi-American Money Plot* (New York: Delacorte Press, 1983).

4. For many fascinating details about the use of atomic bombs against Japan, see Kevin Rafferty II, Jayne Loader, and Pierce Rafferty, film directors, *The Atomic Café*, New Video Group, 2002/1982.

5. Accessing the complete Grimmett Report requires special permission and probably a background check; requests for permission to read the report must be placed through a member of Congress. However, various scholars have read and summarized the report. Nonetheless, one of the best overviews of post–World War II CIA activities extending beyond the Grimmett Report is William Blum, *Killing*

Hope: U.S. Military and C.I.A. Interventions Since World War II (Monroe, ME: Common Courage Press, updated edition, 2004).

6. For details, see Philip Oxhorn, "From Allende to Lula: Assessing the Legacy," *North American Congress on Latin America Report on the Americas* 37, no. 1 (July/August 2003):10, 42 and Nathaniel Davis, *The Last Years of Salvador Allende* (Ithaca, NY: Cornell University Press, 1985), 268–70.

7. Blum, *Killing Hope*, 246–47.

8. See Ayad Allavi, "How Iraq's Elections Set Back Democracy," *The New York Times*, November 2, 2007, A-27.

9. Evidence linking any groups to the 9/11 terrorists is conspicuously absent from the government's *9/11 Report*.

10. For details about Taliban resilience and growth, see Michael J. Sullivan III, *American Adventurism Abroad: Invasions, Interventions, and Regime Changes Since World War II*, Revised and Expanded Edition (Malden, MA: Blackwell Publishing, 2008), 231. For a general account of public opinion about, and perception of, the Taliban during the first years of the American war in Afghanistan, see part two of Anne Nivat's *The Wake of War: Encounters with the People of Iraq and Afghanistan* (Boston: Beacon Press, 2005).

11. For an interesting comparison of the fabrications of threat leading to the Vietnam war and the latest Iraq war, see Gareth Porter, "Manufacturing the Threat to Justify Aggressive War in Vietnam and Iraq," in Lloyd C. Gardner and Marilyn B. Young, eds., *Iraq and the Lessons of Vietnam: Or How **Not** to Learn from the Past* (New York: The New Press, 2007), 88–105.

12. For many of the disheartening details of the American occupation of Iraq, see Rajiv Chandrasekaran, *Imperial Life in the Emerald City: Inside Iraq's Green Zone* (New York: Alfred A. Knopf, 2006).

13. Blum, *Killing Hope*, 392.

14. This point is made more eloquently in Vijay Prashad, *The Darker Nations: A People's History of the Third World* (New York: W.W. Norton and Company, 2007), 279.

15. See the *Global Footprint Network: Advancing the Science of Sustainability* at www.footprintnetwork.org/index.php. Related is the ecological footprint of U.S. carbon dioxide emissions which are five times the rate of the world as a whole and impose huge costs (in the form of global warming damage) borne mostly by third worlders. If all the world produced carbon dioxide at the rate Americans do, we would need nine Earths to deal with it. For details, see "Fighting Climate Change: Human Solidarity in a Divided World," *Human Development Report 2007/2008* (New York: United Nations Development Programme, 2007).

16. John Perkins, *Confessions of an Economic Hit Man* (New York: Plume, 2005).

17. For many more examples and details, see: Kevin Bates, *Disposable People: New Slavery in the Global Economy*, 2nd ed. (Berkeley: University of California Press, 2004).

Postscript: Is America Reparable?

So what do we do about all this trouble? One thing is for certain: knowing what needs to be changed is a lot easier than knowing how to go about trying to change things. The root of the trouble with America lies at the core of our institutional political structures, in the political and economic philosophies upon which our governing system rests. Since pluralism, constitutionalism, and capitalism are our undoing, rectifying the trouble is, at least conceptually, a simple matter of dismantling these structural arrangements in favor of a far more democratic, majoritarian, and socialist political order. It almost doesn't matter what the exact details of such a change might be—whether the majoritarianism be provided by a parliamentary democracy with proportional representation or in some other way; whether the socialism be attained with progressive taxation, autogestion, or greater government ownership. Any move toward a more majoritarian and socialist polity would be a vast improvement over what we have now.

And yet it is exceedingly difficult to imagine such a movement being possible any time soon. The one thing our political structure is really successful at doing is imposing gridlock and preventing meaningful change. If it is virtually impossible for our government to generate substantive public solutions to routine public problems, how could it be possible to do something that entails a major and radical departure from the system of politics itself? Ours is not a political system that lends itself to change. With its hallmark trait being an incapacity to generate much meaningful change in almost any direction, our governing system is perhaps instead a polity that is destined to ultimate collapse, but only when the problems we face have gone inadequately addressed for so long that they overwhelm both us and our pluralist government. Through his carefully designed Constitution,

Madison guaranteed that our government would be exceedingly unlikely to kill its own citizens. At the same time, however, he virtually guaranteed that one day our *problems*, unmitigated and allowed to fester and grow with the absence of effective governmental response, might be our undoing instead.

It is hard to imagine positive change coming from any collapse of the American political system. First of all, genuine crisis does not generally elicit the best of human behavior. Desperate times may call for desperate measures but desperate measures are generally wrought with difficulty and danger. More troubling still is the fact that American history is filled with a long and powerful anti-leftist tradition. If America's political center collapses, it is the political right that is likely to have every advantage in assuming power. It is relatively easy to imagine a "temporary" martial law or "emergency" military rule fueled by anti-minority and xenophobic fears; it is much harder to imagine an American political turn toward socialist democracy, especially in the context of great calamity that would likely accompany the scope of problems capable of forcing our political structures to simply fail to endure any longer.

While scoundrels may hope, plot, and plan for an eventual rightist American dictatorship, what are the well intended to do? Like everyone else, I don't have any compelling answers to such a difficult question but I can refer you to a few of the "what we should do" claims that, over the years, I have found to be at least stirring if not fully inspirational. First, there are the words of novelist A. Anatoli Kuznetsov who, in "a word from the author," interrupts his novel's heart wrenching account of the atrocities of Babi Yar, the Ukrainian ravine where roughly 34,000 people, overwhelmingly Jews, were rounded up, shot, and dumped by Nazi soldiers in the course of two days during World War II (it was also the site of tens of thousands of other Nazi murders in the months that followed). Kuznetsov interrupts his novel to caution us to pay attention to politics:

> How pleasant it is, after all: to treat politics of whatever kind with utter contempt, to dance, to love, to drink and sleep and breathe. To live. God give you strength!
> The only thing is that I can see from my little window that while some people are loving and sleeping, others are busy making handcuffs for them . . .
> Careful my friends!
> On the basis of my own and other people's experience and of experience generally, on the basis of much thinking and searching, worry and calculation, I say to you: THE PERSON WHO TODAY IGNORES POLITICS WILL REGRET IT.
> I did not say I liked politics. I hate them. I scorn them. I do not call upon you to like them or even respect them. I am simply telling you: DON'T IGNORE THEM.[1]

It has been many years since I was first moved by these words. I have been watching politics and politicians ever since. In fact, I have made something of a career of it. As a professor, I have helped countless others watch politics and politicians. And yet I'm not sure what good it does to watch. I am often forewarned of ills that are coming but I can't think of a single time that this has enabled me to prevent them. Besides, in America, the greatest source of trouble is not any group of politicians but, rather, the political system in and of itself, which can thwart the best of intentions from anyone and turn them into gridlock or worse. Kuznetsov's insight seems to imply that the core of our political problem lies with lack of information or awareness. However, in the United States, while there may be huge numbers of people who are uninformed and/or in convenient denial, a bigger problem may be that we are suffering a moral and political paralysis. We know that what our government is doing is fundamentally inadequate in addressing our needs and that it is positively brutal in its treatment of foreigners. What we don't know is what to do about it.

If observation alone is no guarantee of success, maybe it just needs to be combined with thoughtful political activism. Consider these famous words from anthropologist Margaret Mead: "Never doubt that a small group of thoughtful, committed people can change the world; indeed it is the only thing that ever has!"[2] These are indeed motivating words. At the risk of nitpicking, though, I wonder if she means what she inadvertently seems to be suggesting: that neither a single person nor a large group can ever change the world. That doesn't seem right. More worrisome still is the realization that just because small groups can and have effected change at times, doesn't mean that they always can. Thoughtful, committed people may be behind many of the positive changes that have been made but, at other times, perhaps parts of the world are just not very amenable to change.

Novelist and activist Arundhati Roy also offers poignant words of hope for the future. She sees the American people as the source of hope for an end to the imperialism that devastates so much of the world:

> The battle to reclaim democracy is going to be difficult. Our freedoms were not granted to us by any government. They were wrested from them by us. And once we surrender them, the battle to retrieve them is called a revolution. It is a battle that must range across continents and countries. It must not acknowledge national boundaries, but if it is to succeed, it has to begin here. In America. The only institution more powerful than the U.S. government is American civil society. The rest of us are subjects of slave nations. We are by no means powerless, but you have the power of proximity. You have access to the Imperial Palace and the Emperor's chambers. Empire's conquests are being carried out in your name, and you have the right to refuse . . .

Hundreds of thousands of you have survived the relentless propaganda you have been subjected to, and are actively fighting your own government. In the ultra-patriotic climate that prevails in the United States, that's as brave as any Iraqi or Afghan or Palestinian fighting for his homeland.

If you join the battle, not in your hundreds of thousands, but in your millions, you will be greeted joyously by the rest of the world . . .

I hate to disagree with your president. Yours is by no means a great nation. But you could be a great people.

History is giving you the chance.

Seize the time.[3]

Can we Americans save the world after all? What an exciting prospect! And yet, I must admit that Roy's exciting words depressed me. If the world largely depends upon Americans for its easiest path to salvation, the world is in serious trouble.

We Americans are not in much condition to save ourselves, let alone everyone else. Perhaps I know America better than Roy does. We Americans have been horribly damaged by our pluralism and our capitalism. Our pluralism has devastated our ability to fathom that either government or collective action can produce positive results. Under pluralist conditions, they generally can't. Almost all of us falsely believe that freedom emanates from our constitution, not realizing its weaknesses, not realizing that true freedom only comes from empowered, not weakened, communities committed to genuine democracy. In tandem with capitalism, our lack of community has rendered us an overly materialist people. Far too many of us are, at various levels of awareness, deathly afraid of the end of our empire. What Roy seeks may indeed eventually transpire, but I can't escape that feeling that she has just appealed for help from Johnny Rocco.

It is accurate to say that we are indeed caught in a kind of paralysis—highly disillusioned and lacking in both hope and perception of alternatives. In such an environment, it may be only more paralyzing to ask Americans to save the world. As well intended as that may be, we need to think smaller, create little expectation of any immediate or prompt success, and simply ask people to do the right thing.

Even still, when we do the right thing, it will not always be possible to know if we are indeed making things better. For example, those who resisted the Vietnam War did so with seemingly great effect. But did it expedite the end of the war? It is just as plausible that it actually *delayed* the war's end, since the intense disagreement over the war dramatically raised the political stakes of the issue. Those who brought the nation to war were afraid of the domestic political fallout of admitting error and defeat perhaps far more than they feared the stakes in their global struggle against communism. It is possible that doing the right thing can make matters worse rather than better. It will rarely be possible to know what precise effects will be created but somehow it seems only humane to do the right thing anyway.

It may be a mistake to worry too much about outcomes. On a personal level, doing the right thing may be even more important than winning a better world. Upon our deathbeds, who would judge oneself by what she or he won? To seek meaning in life on the basis of political victories may be as much a fool's errand as seeking meaning on the basis of the spaciousness of one's house or the niftiness of one's high definition television. A better measure of our integrity may include how much we care about the well-being of others. Caring would seem to include trying to recognize the needs and interests of the oppressed, and having the courage to act upon what we come to realize is right and humane. While defeat is not to be celebrated, trying to achieve what is difficult and gaining little or no tangible success may be a better endeavor than seeking only what is expedient and doing so with regular success. Our best role models failed far more often than they prevailed and yet, in both their many failures and limited successes, they enhanced our understanding of morality, justice, and humanity.

So what can we do? We can and should speak out often and loudly against our country's horrific military aggressions. While boycotts do not generally work and capitalism is not optional (in other words, we can't choose to go to socialist stores instead), we can at least try to avoid doing business with the most abusive enterprises: the Evil Marts and Evil R Us's of the world. Realizing its limited effects, we can minimize our needless consumption of resource and try to find more solace in one another and less in petty materialism. We can support free trade enterprises, not because it will change the world but simply because it does less harm than the alternative. Mostly, we just need to become far more generous to the needy. We can wring our hands about the want of meaningful choices in our elections but far more useful in such instances, at least in the handful of states that still allow political party cross endorsements, would be participating in, or simply voting for, fusion parties (like the Working Families Party), which endorse only Democrats or Republicans committed to pro-social change of one sort or another, only occasionally running "third" candidates.[4] None of these things, however, useful as they are, will on their own or in combination, save us.

Yes, the American political system is designed to resist change and it does this extremely well. It is a political system that seems destined to eventually collapse. The exact time and circumstance of such a collapse may be impossible to gauge. A global depression brought on by one unaddressed problem or another? Yet another and far worse terrorist attack brought on by continuous foreign policy aggressions? Something else? It's impossible to know. One thing seems likely, however: those of us who champion genuine democracy in America need to be better organized now for the many little battles we are unlikely to win, so we will be better organized for an eventual struggle over what kind of polity we will create when our current one does eventually collapse. *That* will be a struggle we dare not lose. The true test of character, for a nation or an individual, may be behavior in a time of crisis. In such crisis, fear and the prevalence of racism and anti-leftism in America's political culture will put the well intended at every disadvantage. Our only principal advantage will be the country's professed ideals of democracy and freedom. If the overwhelming majority of Americans come to see that the failure of our government comes not from these two values themselves, but from our pluralist, constitutionalist, and capitalist abuses of them, there will indeed be much hope for America and the world. In the very, very long run, we have many reasons to be optimistic. Our planet provides us with sufficient resource and our human character endows us with sufficient imagination and intelligence for us, as a species, to be able to eventually build a prosperous and democratic world. But wouldn't it be wonderful if, in the much nearer term, America becomes a facilitator of, rather than obstacle to, the pursuit of such a world?

NOTES

1. A. Anotoli Kuznetsov, *Babi Yar: A Document in the Form of a Novel*, tr. David Floyd, (New York: Pocket Books, 1971), 44–45.

2. This is almost certainly the most famous quote attributed to Margaret Mead but there is no firm citation for it. Mead is generally believed to have made the remark orally in the presence of the press but there is no currently known early newspaper report citing the quote. Among the earliest textual attributions of these words to Mead is Donald Keys, *Earth at Omega: Passage to Planetization* (Boston: Branden Press, 1982), 79 and references in the *Aiken* (South Carolina) *Standard*, August 5, 1986 and the *Christian Science Monitor*, June 1, 1989.

3. Arundhati Roy, *An Ordinary Person's Guide to Empire* (Cambridge, MA: South End Press, 2004), 66–68.

4. In the late 19th century the Republican party began a successful state to state campaign to illegalize political party cross endorsement, which allowed third parties to seek influence by endorsing on the ballot the Democrat or Republican they preferred, thereby making clear what percentage of that candidate's vote was due to their support. The minor party won genuine influence as a result. The threat to withhold endorsement (and run their own candidate) or to switch endorsement to the other major party's candidate was a significant one, yielding genuine influence. The Republican campaign to illegalize cross endorsement was a direct reaction to the marginal but significant successes of the Populist Party and that party's tendency to mostly support, help elect, and pressure leftward Democrats, much like the Working Families Party now does in New York and Connecticut.

Bibliography

Achebe, Chinua. *The Trouble with Nigeria*. London: Heinemann, 1984.

Adams, Michael C. C. *The Best War Ever: America and World War II*. Baltimore: Johns Hopkins University Press, 1994.

Allavi, Ayad. "How Iraq's Elections Set Back Democracy," *New York Times*, November 2, 2007, A-27.

Appleby, Paul H. *Morality and Administration in Democratic Government*. Baton Rouge, LA: Louisiana State University Press, 1952.

———. *Policy and Administration*. Tuscaloosa, AL: University of Alabama Press, 1949.

Bates, Kevin. *Disposable People: New Slavery in the Global Economy*. 2nd ed. Berkeley: University of California Press, 2004.

Baudrillard, Jean. *America*. trans. Chris Turner. London: Verso, 1988.

Blackmon, Douglas A. *Slavery by Another Name: The Re-Enslavement of Black Americans from the Civil War to World War II*. New York: Doubleday, 2008.

Blum, William. *Killing Home: U.S. Military and C.I.A. Interventions Since World War II*. Updated edition. Monroe, ME: Common Courage Press, 2004.

Bogle, John C. *The Battle for the Soul of Capitalism*. New Haven: Yale University Press, 2005.

Buchan, James. *The Authentic Adam Smith: His Life and Ideas*. New York: Norton, 2006.

Burns, James MacGregor. *Leadership*. New York: Harper and Row, 1978.

Chafe, William. *The Unfinished Journey: America Since World War II*. 5th ed. New York: Oxford University Press, 2003.

Chandrasekaran, Rajiv. *Imperial Life in the Emerald City: Inside Iraq's Green Zone*. New York: Alfred A. Knopf, 2006.

Center for Global Prosperity. *Index of Global Philanthropy*. Washington, D.C.: Center for Global Prosperity, 2007.

Central Intelligence Agency. *The CIA World Factbook, 2007*. New York: Skyhorse Publishing, 2006.

118   *Bibliography*

Centre for International Crime Prevention. *Seventh United Nations Survey of Crime Trends & Operations of Criminal Justice Systems.* New York: United Nations Office on Drugs and Crime, 2007.

Collins, Chuck. *Born on Third Base: The Sources of Wealth of the 1996 Forbes 400.* Boston: United for a Fair Economy, 1997.

Collins, Jim. *Good to Great: Why Some Companies Make the Leap and Others Don't.* New York: Harper Business, 2001.

Corat, Miles, and Wen-Hao Chen. *Child Poverty in Rich Countries, 2005.* Florence, Italy: UNICEF Innocenti Research Centre, 2005.

Dahl, Robert. *Who Governs?* 9th ed. New Haven: Yale University Press, 1979.

Davis, Nathaniel. *The Last Years of Salvador Allende.* Ithaca, NY: Cornell University Press, 1985.

Domhoff, G. William. *Who Rules America: Power and Politics.* 4th ed. Boston: McGraw-Hill, 2002.

Fellner, Jamie, and Marc Mauer. "Losing the Vote: The Impact of Felon Disenfranchisement Laws in the United States." Washington, D.C.: Human Rights Watch and The Sentencing Project, 1998.

Global Footprint Network. "Global Footprint Network: Advancing the Science of Sustainability." 2007. http://www.footprintnetwork.org/index.php. (accessed March 29, 2008).

Hamilton, Alexander, James Madison, and John Jay. *The Federalist Papers.* Edited by Clinton Rossiter. New York: Mentor, 1999.

Herbert, Lenese C. "Bête Noire: How Race-Based Policing Threatens National Security." *Michigan Journal of Race and Law* 9 (2003): 149–213.

———. "Can't You See What I'm Saying? Making Expressive Conduct a Crime in High Crime Areas." *Georgetown Journal on Poverty Law & Policy* 9, no. 135 (2002): 138–45.

Hersh, Seymour M. *Chain of Command: The Road from 9/11 to Abu Ghraib.* New York: HarperCollins, 2004.

Higham, Charles. *Trading with the Enemy: An Exposé of the Nazi-American Money Plot.* New York: Delacorte Press, 1983.

Horwitz, Morton J. *The Transformation of American Law, 1780–1860.* Cambridge: Harvard University Press, 1977.

———. *The Transformation of American Law, 1870–1960.* New York: Oxford University Press, 1992.

Hoy, Michael. "Jon Alpert: NBC's Odd Man Out." *Columbia Journalism Review* 30, no. 3 (September 1991): 44–47.

International Institute for Democracy and Electoral Assistance. *Voter Turnout: A Global Survey.* Stolkholm: International IDEA, 1998.

Inter-Parliamentary Union. *Women in National Parliaments.* Geneva, Switzerland: Inter-Parliamentary Union, 2007. http://www.ipu.org/wmn-e/classif.htm (accessed March, 2008).

Irons, Peter. *A People's History of the Supreme Court.* New York: Penguin, 1999.

Jäntti, Markus, Bernt Bratsberg, Knut Röed, Oddbjörn Raaum, Robin Naylor, Eva Österbacka, Anders Björklund, and Tor Eriksson. "American Exceptionalism in a New Light: A Comparison of Intergenerational Earnings Mobility in the Nordic

Countries, United Kingdom and the United States." Discussion Paper No. 1938. Bonn, Germany: Institute for the Study of Labor, 2006.

Keys, Donald. *Earth at Omega: Passage to Planetization.* Boston: Branden Press, 1982.

Kuznetsov, A. Anotoli. *Babi Yar: A Document in the Form of a Novel.* Trans. David Floyd. New York: Pocket Books, 1971.

Lawler, Edward E. III. *The Ultimate Advantage: Creating the High Involvement Organization.* San Francisco: Jossey-Bass Publishers, 1992.

Levine, David I., and Laura D'Andrea Tyson. "Participation, Productivity, and the Firm's Environment." In *Paying for Productivity: A Look at the Evidence.* Edited by Alan S. Blinder. Washington, D.C.: Brookings Institution, 1990.

Lipsitz, George. *The Possessive Investment in Whiteness: How White People Profit from Identity Politics.* Philadelphia: Temple University Press, 1998.

Locke, John. Second Treatise of Government. Edited by C. B. Macpherson. Indianapolis: Hackett Publishing Co., 1980/1690.

Long, Kenneth J. "No Good Wars: Teaching the History of Modern Wars as a Means of Resisting Current Ones." *College Teaching* 55 no. 2 (Winter 2008): 1–7.

Lowi, Theodore J. *The End of Liberalism.* 2nd ed. New York: Norton, 1979.

Madison, James. "Federalist Paper Number 10." In Alexander Hamilton, James Madison, and John Jay. *The Federalist Papers.* Edited by Clinton Rossiter. New York: Mentor, 1999.

———. "Federalist Paper Number 51." In Alexander Hamilton, James Madison, and John Jay. *The Federalist Papers.* Edited by Clinton Rossiter. New York: Mentor, 1999.

Marx, Karl. *The Economic and Philosophical Manuscripts of 1844.* Amherst, NY: Oxford University Press, 2000/1956.

Mishel, Lawrence, Jared Bernstein, and Sylvia Allegretto. *The State of Working America 2006/2007.* Ithaca, NY: ILR Press.

Mishel, Lawrence, Jared Bernstein, and John Schmitt. *The State of Working America 2000/2001.* Ithaca, NY: ILR Press, 2001.

Mitchell, Peter R., and John Schoeffel, eds. *Understanding Power: The Indispensable Chomsky.* New York: The New Press, 2002.

Moore, Robert, David Gahl, Tim Sweeney, and Jackson Morris. *Wasted Green: How Lost Revenue and State Spending Shortchange New York Taxpayers & the Environment.* Albany, NY: Environmental Advocates of New York, 2008.

Morrison, Toni. *Playing in the Dark: Whiteness and the Literary Imagination.* New York: Vintage Books, 1993/1992.

National Commission on Terrorist Attacks. *The 9/11 Commission Report: Final Report of the National Commission on Terrorist Attacks upon the United States.* New York: Norton & Co., 2004.

Nivat, Anne. *The Wake of War: Encounters with the People of Iraq and Afghanistan.* Boston: Beacon Press, 2005.

Organization for Economic Cooperation and Development. *Employment Outlook.* Paris: OECD, 1996.

Oxhorn, Philip. "From Allende to Lula: Assessing the Legacy." *North American Congress on Latin America Report on the Americas* 37, no. 1 (July/August 2003): 9–13, 42.

Perkins, John. *Confessions of an Economic Hit Man.* New York: Plume, 2005.

Porter, Gareth. "Manufacturing the Threat to Justify Aggressive War in Vietnam and Iraq." In *Iraq and the Lessons of Vietnam: Or How Not to Learn from the Past.* Edited by Lloyd C. Gardner and Marilyn B. Young. New York: The New Press, 2007.

Prashad, Vijay. *The Darker Nations: A People's History of the Third World.* New York: W.W. Norton and Company, 2007.

Rafferty, Kevin II, Jayne Loader, and Pierce Rafferty, film directors. *The Atomic Café.* New Video Group, 2002/1982.

Roy, Arundhati. *An Ordinary Person's Guide to Empire.* Cambridge, MA: South End Press, 2004.

Schuman, David F., with Bob Waterman. *A Preface to Politics.* 4th ed. Lexington, MA: DC Heath & Co., 1986.

Schuman, David F., and Rex Wirth. *A Preface to Politics.* 6th ed. Novato, CA: Chandler & Sharp, 2004.

Scrammon, Richard M., and Ben J. Wattenberg. *The Real Majority.* New York: Coward-McCann Publishers, 1970.

Smeeding, Timothy M. "Financial Poverty in Developed Countries: The Evidence from LIS." Luxembourg Income Study Working Paper No. 155, 1997.

Sullivan, Michael III, *American Adventurism Abroad: Invasions, Interventions, and Regime Changes Since World War II.* Revised and Expanded Edition. Malden, MA: Blackwell Publishing, 2008.

Tocqueville, Alexis de. *Democracy in America.* Vol. 1. Edited by Phillips Bradley. New York: Knopf, 1945/1835.

Uchitte, Louis. "The Richest of the Rich, Proud of a New Guilded Age." *New York Times,* July 15, 2007, 1, 20–21.

United Nations Development Programme. "Fighting Climate Change: Human Solidarity in a Divided World," *Human Development Report 2007/2008.* New York: United Nations Development Programme, 2007.

———. *Human Development Report 2007/2008.* New York: Palgrave Macmillan, 2007.

Wattenburg, Martin P. *Where Have All the Voters Gone?* Cambridge: Harvard University Press, 2002.

Wolff, Robert Paul. *The Poverty of Liberalism.* Boston: Beacon Press, 1968.

World Health Organization. *The World Health Report 2000, Health Systems.* Geneva: World Health Organization, 2000.

Zagorsky, Jay L. "Do You Have to be Smart to be Rich? The Impact of IQ on Wealth, Income and Financial Distress." *Intelligence* 35, no. 5 (September/October 2007): 489–501.

Zinn, Howard. *A People's History of the United States 1492–Present.* New York: Perennial Classics, 2001.

Index

dependency theory, 107
de Tocqueville, Alexis, 28, 32, 74
development projects, 71, 86n10, 108
Diem, Ngo Dinh, 98
domestic policy, xxxix–xxxv, 61–62,
    114; and abdication of
    responsibility, 83–85; and
    American political culture, 69–76;
    leadership, representation, and,
    76–83; and localism and
    federalism, 67–69; and subsidizing
    the rich more than the poor,
    65–67; and tax policy, 62–65
Dominican Republic, 99
Dresden, 92
dual sovereignty, 10
due process clause, 34–35
Duke, David, 82
Dulles, Allen, 95

ecological footprint, 106–7, 110n15
economy, xxxiii–xxxiv, xxxv, xxxvi, 5,
    11, 27, 40, 44, 45, 48–50, 52,
    55–56, 74–75, 105
economy of scale, 56, 66
Ecuador, 93, 95
education, xviii, xxi–*xxiii*, xxviii, xxxi,
    15, 20, 35, 45, 47, 50, 57n5, 61, 67,
    74, 79, 83–84
Edwards, Edwin, 82
Edwards, John, xiii
efficiency, xxxii, 40–44, 47, 56–57, 69
Egypt, 70, 86n9, 99
election system, xxvi–xxviii, xxxi, 10,
    19, 27, 70, 78–83, 86–87n19, 98,
    100, 115
elite theory, 20, 41
Ellis Island, 71–72
El Salvador, 99
Employment Security Act of 1974
    (Sweden), 27
Enron scandal, 42
Espionage Act of 1917 and 1918, 25
eugenics, 71, 72, 91
Europe, xviii–xx, 19, 31, 32, 33, 42, 44,
    47, 61, 63, 64, 66, 71, 72, 74, 83,
    84, 91, 92, 105. *See also* British

empire; Denmark; Finland;
    Germany; Greece; Italy; Norway;
    Russia; Serbia; Sweden; Ukraine
European Union, 19
executive branch, 9, 10, 12, 14, 19, 25,
    26, 32, 64, 70, 71, 79, 81,
    86–87n19, 89, 91, 96, 114
executive orders, 12
externalities, 42–43

faction, 6–7, 9, 11, 12
Fairchild, Mark, 82
Farrakhan, Louis, 73
fascism, 45, 70, 73, 82, 86n11, 89, 93,
    94, 95, 96, 98, 104. *See also
    particular fascist leaders and countries*
Federal Bureau of Investigation (FBI),
    25, 32
federalism, 67–69; defined, xxxiii, 10.
    See also checks and balances;
    pluralism
Federalist Papers. *See* Madison, James
felon exclusion laws, 50, 73, 81
feminism, xx–xxi, 50
Figueres, José, 96
filibuster, 13
Finland, xx, xxiv, 58n10, 66
First Amendment, 24–25, 29, 32. *See
    also* speech rights
flag, 84
flat tax, 63–64, 103
Florida, 81, 86–87n19
Ford Motor Company, 91, 106
foreign policy, xii, xxxvi, 62, 69, 70–71,
    76, 86n10, 115; and blocking, or
    meddling with, democracies, 99;
    contemporary, 89–90; and creating
    or supporting false democracies,
    99–100; and failed attempts to
    overthrow democracies, 96–97;
    history up to and through World
    War II, 90–93; and imperialism,
    105–9; and Korean War, 97–98; and
    overthrowing democracies, 93–96;
    and Vietnam War, 98–99; and wars
    in Afghanistan and Iraq, 100–104
Fourteenth Amendment, 25, 34–35

media, 7, 14, 23, 24, 28, 32–33, 109, 116n2
melting pot, 70, 72–73
Mexican-American War, 73–74
Mexico, 73–74, 90, 106
Middle East. *See* Africa; Asia
military coups, xxxi, xxxii, 23, 93–97, 99, 107, 108
military regimes, xxviii, xxxi–xxxii, 94–99, 108, 112
Millennium Development Goals (MDG), 71, 86n10
Mills, C. Wright, 20
minority rights, 8, 13, 14, 15, 36, 65, 73, 81, 104, 112
Mississippi, 50, 73
mobility, xxiii, *xxiv–xxv*, 15, 47–48, 51, 58, 65, 72, 73, 90. *See also* opportunity
Mobutu Sese Seko, 95
money, xxvi, xxviii, xxxii, 5, 12–13, 26, 35, 39, 40–41, 43, 45, 46, 52, 62, 65–66, 72, 97, 108. *See also* currency
Morrison, Toni, 86n12
Mossadegh, Mohammad, 93–94, 107
motivation: economic, 41, 45, 47; political, 93, 100, 101, 102, 107, 113
multi-party system. *See* election system
multiple member districts. *See* election system
murder, xx–*xxi*, 17, 23, 32, 51, 52, 72, 95, 96, 97, 98, 100, 112
Murdoch, Rupert, 32
Musharraf, Pervez, 102
My Lai massacre, 99

Nagasaki, 92
National Liberation Front, 98
Native Americans, xxxv, 56; genocide, 37n1, 74–75, 90
Nazi Germany, 37n1, 61, 91–93, 108, 112
neo-conservatives. *See* conservatives
New Deal, 83
New Hampshire, 77
New Haven Study. *See* Dahl, Robert

New Jersey plan, 10
New York, 6, 26, 29, 33, 43, 57n7, 72, 82, 116n4
Nicaragua, 97
Nigeria, xxvii, xxxi–xxxvii
Nixon, Richard, 25, 81, 83, 93, 95–96
non-responsible party system. *See* election system
North Korea, 97–98
Northern Alliance, 101
Norway, 58n10

Obama, Barack, xiii
Obasanjo, Olusegun, xxxi
oil, xxviii, xxxii, 41–42, 43, 93, 102, 106, 107
oligopoly, 42, 55
Omaha Beach, 92
open society, 29, 40, 44, 70–71, 77
opportunity, xviii, xxiii, *xxiv–xxv*, xxviii, xxxv, 20, 35, 44, 47–49, 51, 55, 56, 61, 65, 70, 71, 73, 84. *See also* mobility
Organization for Economic Co-operation and Development (OECD), xxiv, 86n10
Ortega, Daniel, 97

Pahlavi, Mohammed Reza (Shah of Iran), 93–94
Pakistan, 101–2
Palestinians, 99, 114
Panama (invasion of), 37n1
Papadopoulos, Georgios, 95
Papandreou, Andreas, 95
Papandreou, George, 95
paralysis, xii, 114. *See also* gridlock; pluralism; power vacuums; weakness of government
parliamentary democracy, 4, 19, 45, 93–94, 111
PATRIOT Act, 24–25, 37
Pearl Harbor, 91
Perkins, John, 107–8
Philippines, 90, 91, 99
Pinkertons, 26
Pinochet, Augusto, 96, 107